ROMANCE MONOGRAPHS, INC.
Number 39

# LOVE'S FATAL GLANCE:
## A STUDY OF EYE IMAGERY IN THE POETS OF THE
## *ECOLE LYONNAISE*

ROMANCE MONOGRAPHS, INC.
Number 39

# LOVE'S FATAL GLANCE:
## A STUDY OF EYE IMAGERY IN THE POETS OF THE *ECOLE LYONNAISE*

BY

LANCE K. DONALDSON-EVANS

UNIVERSITY, MISSISSIPPI
ROMANCE MONOGRAPHS, INC.
1980

**Library of Congress Cataloging in Publication Data**

Donaldson-Evans, Lance K
    Love's fatal glance.

    (Romance monographs; no. 39)
    Bibliography: p.

    1. French poetry—16th century—History and criticism. 2. French poetry—France—Lyons—History and criticism. 3. Love poetry, French—History and criticism. 4. Eye in literature. 5. French language—Figures of speech. I. Title.

PQ418.D6          841'.3'09354          80-10415

# TABLE OF CONTENTS

# INTRODUCTION

THIS STUDY IS, at least in part, the answer to a question once directed to me by an undergraduate student during a class discussion on sixteenth century French love poetry. The question was a simple request for information as to the origin of the metaphor which depicts the Lady's eyes as shooting arrows in order to inspire love in the Beholder. When I replied that this image was of course a Petrarchan cliché, my questioner was quick to pursue her line of thought and went on to ask from which source Petrarch himself was drawing. The answer to this second enquiry proved to be far more elusive. I was, I confessed, at a loss and promised further elucidation in a subsequent class. After some considerable time spent researching the question, I had to admit defeat, for no one had satisfactorily traced the image back from the French Renaissance love poets to its probable origins. It was then that I decided to undertake this investigation. For this reason, the first section of the present study attempts to retrace the history of the type of eye imagery which puzzled my student, and provides, I trust, a more satisfactory answer to her questions than I was previously able to give.

The major part of this study, which deals with the Lyonnais poets, emerged from a discovery which came to light during my research into the history of the metaphor depicting the eye as an archer. To my surprise, I learned that, in spite of the frequency of eye imagery in sixteenth century French love poetry, most critics only mention it in passing and have little or nothing to say about the eyes' role in engendering and nurturing love.

The importance attributed to the eyes as messengers and inspirers of love is prevalent throughout the sixteenth century in

France and to do justice to its richness, one would need to study
the vast corpus of love poetry which extends from the Grands Rhé-
toriqueurs to Aggrippa D'Aubigné. I have chosen to limit the scope
of this essay (essay in Montaigne's sense) to the Lyonnais poets,
because they were the first group of French Renaissance writers to
make frequent and consistent use of this type of eye imagery so
that it became not just an oft-repeated commonplace, but an integral part of their treatment of love. These poets, chronologically
at the vanguard of the French Renaissance, and geographically at
the cultural and commercial crossroads which Lyons represented
in sixteenth century France, have received relatively little critical
attention compared with that accorded to the writers of the Pléiade,
so that a study of their eye imagery also elucidates certain neglected
aspects of their love poetry and reveals more clearly their role in
the development of French Renaissance poetry.

There are many people to thank for their advice and help at
various stages of this project: Professors Jean Rousset and Jean
Starobinski of the University of Geneva for their counsel, the latter
in particular for orienting me towards the medical and philosophical
background of Renaissance eye imagery (including the works of
Jacques Ferrand); my colleagues Clifton Cherpack, whose knowledge of the Greek Romance helped me to discover how such authors
as Heliodorus and Achilles Tatius used eye imagery in their portrayal of love, Victoria Kirkham and Roger Allen, whose exper-
tise in Italian and Arabic — respectively — love poetry was often
tapped. I am also particularly grateful to the American Council of
Learned Societies for a Summer Grant which enabled me to pursue
my research in Europe. I would also like to express my gratitude
to my colleagues of the Faculty of Arts and Sciences at the University of Pennsylvania, and in particular the former Dean (now
Provost) Vartan Gregorian, for their encouragement and moral sup-
port. Last of all, my deepest thanks are due to my wife for her
help and her patience during my excursions into the dangerous
territory of Renaissance love poetry where one glance from a Lady's
eye can bring love, suffering and death.

# CHAPTER I

# THE EYES' ROLE IN LOVE LITERATURE
## SINCE ANTIQUITY

*Si nescis, oculi sunt in amore duces.* [1]

THE ROLE PLAYED by the eyes in the generation and transmission of love is one of the most pervasive themes in amatory literature and one of the least studied. The importance attributed to the eyes in such literature can, of course, be seen as a fairly obvious literary adaptation of a physiological fact: that in most traditions, love begins when the object of love is perceived by the Lover's eyes. Although falling in love with an unseen and unknown person is a literary motif in its own right, [2] it is considerably less frequent than the tradition which predicates love with sight. Usually it is the Beloved's beauty which engenders love through the medium of the eyes. Indeed this aspect of falling in love appears to be so widespread and so constant in all literature that it is virtually impossible to seek specific sources. However, when love is portrayed as something sudden, irresistible and excruciating at the Lover's first encounter with the Beloved, when love is born not simply as a result of seeing the Beloved but by the active participation of the Beloved's own glance, then we are dealing with a specific tradition which can be traced back to early Greek literature. It is in fact a topos which, since it has gone unnamed until now, we propose to call the aggressive eye topos. It is this topos and its associated imagery which is the principal subject of the present study.

---

[1] Propertius, *Elegia,* lib. II, XV, 1. 12.
[2] See for example *Standard Dictionary of Folklore, Mythology and Legend* (New York: Funk and Wagnall, 1949).

Surprisingly, the vast majority of those critics who have turned their attention to this tradition, have usually limited themselves to pointing out its presence in a particular author's work and have been satisfied with a general statement of the universality of the imagery associated with it. [3] Those who have attempted to be more specific have suggested classical sources, particularly Ovid [4] (the general assumption being that all post-Ovidian love literature must, to some extent at least, be inspired by the *Ars amatoria*) but have gone no further in their investigation. If a post-petrarchan author is under discussion, [5] the reader is in most cases referred to Petrarch himself or to the *dolce stil nuovo*, without further elaboration. In studies on sixteenth century French love poetry which abounds in references to the eyes' aggressive role in the love experience, in most cases we are simply told that we are in the presence of a typically petrarchan or neo-petrarchan (that is, inspired by Bembo, Sasso and so on) theme. It is true that, occasionally, a link with neo-platonism is revealed. For example in Henri Weber's excellent study of French Renaissance poetry, [6] Ficino's *Commentary of Plato's Symposium* is cited as a source of the theme. In fact, despite its immediate influence on Renaissance love literature, Ficino's work is itself only a rather late elaboration of an already well-established literary tradition. The most one can say about the treatment the majority of critics have accorded the aggressive eye topos is that "ils nous laissent sur notre faim."

There have been one or two fortunate exceptions to this disinclination to trace the theme of the eyes' role in love to its probable source. Herbert Kolb, in his study of the medieval courtly lyric, [7] does not of course have petrarchism to fall back on, and so in a short section of his work devoted to "Die Mystik des Auges

---

[3] See for example Mark S. Whitney (ed.), *Les odes amoureuses d'Olivier de Magny* (Geneva: Droz, 1964), who, when commenting on a typical aggressive eye image, has this to say: "[...] Cliché qui se trouve un peu partout chez les poètes favoris de Magny," p. 6.

[4] See Jean Frappier on Chrétien de Troyes, *ALMA,* ed. R. S. Loomis (Oxford, 1959), p. 173.

[5] See Marius Piéri, *Pétrarque et Ronsard* (New York: B. Franklin, 1968), pp. 70 ff.

[6] Henri Weber, *La création poétique au XVIᵉ siècle en France* (Paris: Nizet, 1965).

[7] Herbert Kolb, *Der Begriff der Minne und das Entstehen der höfischen Lyrik* (Tübingen, 1958), particularly pp. 18-38.

und des Herzens," he reviews some of the classical antecedents for attributing a warlike, aggressive character to the Beloved's gaze and for depicting its violating effect on the Lover's own eyes. He traces the theme back to Plato (in particular to the *Timaeus* and *Phaedrus*) and from there forward to Saint Augustine and certain theologians of the Middle Ages. His account is certainly more complete and informative than the more usual neglect of the topos' origins, but it is all too brief and neglects many important aspects of its transmission and development, while attributing undue importance to the medieval theologians, who played a minor part.

The only thorough study made of the aggressive eye motif in love literature is the late Ruth Cline's excellent and well researched "Heart and Eyes," [8] which explores the motif's origins and use from early Greek literature up to Chrétien de Troyes. Although her article approaches the question from a somewhat different perspective from ours (we will focus our attention particularly on the imagery associated with the eyes themselves at the inception of love, while she is interested in the strife which ensues between heart and eyes after the *innamoramento*), her work contains many invaluable insights and we shall have occasion to refer to her findings in subsequent sections of this chapter.

\* \* \*

It should be noted at the outset that the aggressive eye topos is not simply a fanciful metaphor for the suddenness with which love strikes and for the tyranny it exercises over its victim. When the modern reader encounters images which picture the eyes shooting forth arrows or lightning bolts, he or she is often disturbed by their apparent artifice or preciosity. In fact, such imagery is rooted in a theory of vision which extended from classical Antiquity up to the seventeenth century. This scientific authority (it is only for us that it is pseudo-scientific) undoubtedly accounts for the popularity and extraordinary longevity of this · particular literary tradition.

---

[8] Ruth Cline, "Heart and Eyes," *Romance Philology,* vol. 25, 1971-72, pp. 263-297. See also A. C. Pearson, "Phrixus and Demodice," *The Classical Review,* vol. XXIII, 1909, pp. 255-57, a concise note giving many valuable references to the use of eye imagery in Greek literature.

In ancient Greek philosophy, there were two rival schools of thought concerning the means by which the eye is able to see, the principal opponents being, not surprisingly, Plato and Aristotle. Plato's interpretation of the phenomenon of sight opts for an efflux theory of vision [9] and in so doing he aligns himself with Empedokles, although there are differences between the two which would be important to a physicist or a philosopher but which have no literary effect on the topos we are considering. [10] Briefly, the efflux theory of vision represents the eye not as a mere receiver or reflector of light rays, but as possessing its own internal illumination in the form of fire. The eye is described as being a transmitter of light, sending out beams which, when they strike another object, either carry the image back to the eye or actually join the eye to the object being viewed. The eye therefore plays a dynamic role in the act of seeing and becomes an extension of the body from which light is projected. Plato also attributes pre-eminence to sight among the five senses. This is because he believes sight to be intimately related to the soul, and the eyes to be the principal means by which it can acquire knowledge.

The creation of the eyes and their function in the body are described in the *Timaeus*:

> Imitating the shape of the universe, which was spherical, they [the creators] confined the two divine revolutions within a globe-shaped body, the same that we now call the head, which is the divinest part of us and has dominion over all our members. [...] Therefore, having set the face upon the globe of the head on that side, they attached to it organs for all the forethought of the soul, and they ordained that this which had the faculty of guidance should be by nature the front. And first of the organs they wrought light-giving eyes, which they fixed there on the plan I shall explain. Such sort of fire as had the property of yielding a gentle light but not of burning, they contrived to form into a substance akin to the light of every day. The fire within us, which is akin to daylight,

---

[9] See the remarks of H. Blumberg in his edition of Averroes, *Epitome of Parva Naturalia* (Cambridge, 1961), p. 81.

[10] R. D. Archer, in his edition of Plato's *Timaeus* (London, 1888), p. 155 insists that Plato's account of the mechanism of sight is much more subtle and refined than that of Empedokles. However, for our purposes, the transmission of the concept to literature, they may be considered to be identical.

they made to flow pure, smooth and dense through the eyes [...] Whenever then there is daylight surrounding the current of vision, then this issues forth as like into like and coalescing with the light is formed into one uniform substance in the direct line of vision, wherever the stream issuing from within strikes upon some external object that forms in its way. So the whole from its uniformity becomes sympathetic and whenever it comes in contact with anything else, or anything with it, it passes on the notions there-of over the whole body until they reach the soul, and then causes that sensation which we call seeing. [11]

A rival theory of vision propounded by Aristotle in the *De sensu* which challenged Plato's ideas on logical and empirical grounds, denied that the eyes actually projected light and made of them simple receptors of images, thus depriving them of the aggressive and dynamic quality implicitly vested in them by the platonic theory. While the aristotelian concept is obviously much closer to the modern scientific description of vision, the platonic theory managed to co-exist quite healthily with its rival right until the end of the Renaissance and had just as much authority until empirical science proved it to be inaccurate. [12] It also exercised an important influence over both medical thought (at least in Galenic medicine, since Galenus followed Plato's theory of emanation from

---

[11] Plato, op. cit., pp. 155-157. That the basic elements of the Platonic theory still enjoyed "scientific" favour as late as the end of the sixteenth century can be seen in Lomazzo's *Trattato dell'Arte de la Pittura* (Milano, 1584) where we find the following description of the eyes' workings: "I raggi del videre, che sono quelli che partendosi da l'occhio vanno pigliando tutte le particolarita de gl'oggetti che si vogliono dipingere [...] ritornano per diretto a l'occhio d'onde si partirono," p. 259.

[12] It is interesting that during the Italian Renaissance, Leone Ebreo in his *Dialoghi d'Amore* attempted a reconciliation of the two theories which preserves the dynamic quality of Plato's theory: "[...] for I hold that both the transmission of rays from the eye to apprehend and illumine the object and the representation of the form of the object in the pupil are necessary to sight; and further, these two contrary are not sufficient without a third and final notion, namely that the eye directs its rays for a second time on to the object to make the form (impressed on the pupil) tally in every respect with the external object. And in this third action consists the true essence of vision [...] and my purpose is to prove [...] that the eye not only sees but first illumines what is sees." Leone Ebreo, *The Philosophy of Love,* trans. F. Friedeberg-Seeley and Jean H. Barnes (London: The Soncino Press, 1937), p. 215.

the eye, even though he did not subscribe to other elements in the Platonic concept of vision), [13] and literature for many centuries.

Although Plato's theories of vision are important to our understanding of how the Ancients understood the workings of the eye, and while it serves to give a certain scientific and philosophical authenticity to a topos which represents the eye as emitting beams which strike and wound their recipient, Plato is not the initiator of the tradition which makes the eyes not simply receptors of beauty but agents in engendering love. Following Cline's and A. C. Pearson's [14] investigations, the earliest use of it we have been able to uncover is by Hesiod in the 8th century B. C., who in the *Theogony* attributes the power of awakening love to the eyes of the Graces:

> Eurynome, daughter of Okeanos,
> lovely in appearance,
> bore to Zeus the three Graces
> with fair cheeks; they are
> Aglaia and Euphrosyne and lovely Thalia,
> and from the glancing of their lidded eyes
> bewildering
> love distills; there is beauty
> in their glance, from beneath brows. [15]

The first reference in Antiquity to the eye actually casting arrows appears to be in Aeschylus' *Agamemnon*. The image is first applied to Iphigeneia, who, when she is being led out to be sacrificed, tries to instill, not love in this instance, but pity in the hearts of her sacrificers by the power of her glance:

> And she, as she let fall to the ground her saffron-dyed raiment, smote each one of her sacrificers with a pitiful arrow from her eye [...] [16]

Here the dynamic influence of the eye over others is acknowledged, so that later in the play we are not surprised to discover

[13] See Rudolph E. Siegel, *Galen on Sense Perception* (Basel and New York, 1970).
[14] Pearson, op. cit.
[15] Hesiod, *The Works and Days. Theogony,* trans. R. Lattimore (Ann Arbor, 1970), ll. 907 ff., p. 178.
[16] Aeschylus, *Agamemnon,* ed. E. Fraenkel (Oxford, 1950), ll. 240 ff.

Although implicit here, it is obvious that it was Medea's seeing Jason (this is why Eros positions himself "close by Aeson's son") which caused the havoc within her breast. Further on in the *Argonautica* after Jason has asked Medea for the magic charm, it is through the exchange of loving glances between the two that Eros is sure of his prey:

> And forth from her fragrant girdle ungrudgingly she brought out the charm [...] and she would even have drawn out all her soul from her breast and given it to him, exulting in his desire; so wonderfully did love flash forth a sweet flame from the golden head of Aeson's son; and he captivated her gleaming eyes; and her heart within grew warm, melting away as the dew melts away around roses when warmed by the morning's light. And now both were fixing their eyes on the ground abashed, and again were throwing glances at each other, smiling with the light of love beneath their radiant brows [...] [25]

When we look at the poets whose work has been preserved and transmitted through the *Greek Anthology,* we find that still more importance is attributed to the eyes in the love experience. In the works of the first century B. C. poet Meleager, we find the familiar figure of Cupid bearing bow and arrows, but here Cupid is not simply close by the Beloved, as in Apollonius Rhodius, his very lair is in the Beloved's eyes:

> Take care he does not set new snares in your souls! But look! there he is in his lair. I see you little arrow-shooter, hiding in Zenophile's eyes! [26]

In Meleager's poems, the eyes are also transmitters of the flame of love as in Apollonius Rhodius (and Plato). In "Heraclitus and Diodorus," he writes:

> Heraclitus speaks silently with his eyes: "I cast the thunder-fire of Zeus."
> And the breast of Diodorus says: "I melt the stone which is warmed against me."

---

[25] Ibid., ll. 1013 ff.
[26] Meleager, "A Description of Love," in *Medallions from Anyte of Tegea, Meleager of Gadara, The Anacreontea, Latin Poets of the Renaissance,* trans. Richard Aldington (London, 1930), p. 24.

> Unhappy he who is smitten by the flame from the eyes of the one
> and by the soft fire smouldering with desire from the other. [27]

The eyes are also portrayed as traitors to the soul and as being ceaselessly involved in searching out new loves in an epigramme entitled "To His Eyes":

> Eyes, betrayers of the soul, hunters of new loves, ever caught in the snares of Aphrodite, you seize another love [...] [28]

The eyes are also able to wound:

> Myiscus, whose eyes had stabbed me [...] [29]

and to set snares even for the God of Love himself:

> Winged Love, himself is a prisoner in heaven, captured by your eyes, Timarion [...] [30]

In yet another poem the rays projected by the eyes are compared with those of the sun, the eyebeams kindling the fire of passion within the poet's heart:

> At noon I saw Alexis walking in the road when Summer shears the tresses of the wheat.
> Two rays of fire burned me; the first, Love's, from his eyes, the other from the sun which night will soon appease, but in dreams the image of his beauty will but burn me the more.
> Sleep, that brings peace to others, brings pain to me, creating beauty, a living flame in my heart. [31]

This poem is eloquent proof that whatever authority the Aristotelian theory of vision may have exercised in the world of philosophy

---

27 Ibid., p. 39.
28 Ibid., p. 43.
29 Ibid., p. 44.
30 Ibid., p. 45.
31 Ibid., p. 47.

and science, the Platonic efflux theory was the one preferred by poets.

There are similar examples from the Anacreontic poetry of the *Greek Anthology*. In a battle with the God of Love, the poet manages to resist the arrows of Eros only to be conquered by his wounding glance:

> And as he had no shafts he grew angry and hurled himself at me in a glance [. . .] [32]

In a piece entitled a "Portrait of a Lady," another Anacreontic poet writes:

> Make her eyes of real fire, clear like Athene's . . . [33]

and in a poem dedicated to the Lady's eyes we read:

> No horse slew me, no foot-soldier, no ship, but a new enemy struck me from her eyes. [34]

It is apparent then that the primary role given to the eyes in the experience of falling in love is well established in the pre-Christian era of Greek literature and that almost all the imagery associated with the eyes is already present: the eyes shoot arrows, daggers or swords, project fiery beams which burn the soul and kindle love's flame; the eyes are directly associated with Cupid and are often the instrument by which he casts his shafts; the eyes are trappers, ensnaring the unsuspecting glances of others; the glance of love casts a spell, a *fascinatio,* over its victim. Parallel to this cluster of images associated with the working of the eyes in love is the corollary that the eyes of the Beholder are passive receptacles of the aggressive glance, although in some instances they are described as messengers, usually traitorous, going forth from the Beholder, seizing the image of the Beloved's beauty and bringing it back to take up residence within the soul of the Lover. In any case, it is the eyes of the Beholder-Lover which are the gateways

---

[32] Ibid., p. 63.
[33] Ibid., p. 65.
[34] Ibid., p. 70.

to his or her soul and whether actively or passively, willingly or unwillingly, they are the indispensible allies of the Beloved's eyes.

In view of the importance the aggressive eye topos had assumed in pre-christian Greek poetry, it is no surprise to find that it is even more prominent in the Greek romances of the third and fourth centuries (A.D.). In the works of Heliodorus, Longus and Achilles Tatius, this motif is often present in the description of nascent love. In the romance of *Theagenes and Chariclea* by Heliodorus, Charicles, shortly after his daughter has seen Theagenes and fallen in love with him, visits her only to find that she is stricken with a mysterious disease. Her father asks his companion what ails her and when told that perhaps she has been looked upon by some envious eye, professes scepticism at the notion of fascination. His companion then treats us to an interesting defense of this belief and relates it to the process of falling in love:

> "And do you too," he returned, smiling ironically, "think with the vulgar, that there is anything in fascination?" "Indeed I do," said I, "and thus I account for its effects: this air which surrounds us, which we take in with our breath, receive at our eyes and nostrils and which penetrates into all our pores, brings with it those qualities with which it is impregnated; and according to their different natures, we are differently affected. When anyone looks at what is excellent with an envious eye, he fills the surrounding atmosphere with a pernicious quality, and transmits his own envenomed exhalations into whatever is nearest to him. They, as they are thin and subtle, penetrate even into the bones and marrow; and this envy has become the cause of a disorder to many, which has obtained the name of fascination.
>
> Consider besides, O Charicles, how many have been infected with inflammation of the eyes, and with other contagious distempers, without ever touching [...] those who laboured under them, but solely by breathing the same air with them. The birth of love affords another proof of what I am explaining, which, by the eyes alone, finds a passage to the soul; and it is not difficult to assign the reason; for as, of all the inlets to our senses, the sight is the most quick and fiery, and most various in its motives; this animated faculty most easily receives the influences

which surround it, and attracts to itself the emanations of love." [35]

The description continues with examples from natural history, including the famous basilisk mentioned by Pliny. [36] This passage is particularly significant as it shows both the importance its author attributes to the phenomenon of vision in general and in particular to the role the eye plays in inspiring love. It is interesting that many of the details we find in this passage, or variations on them, appear in the works of Renaissance philosophers and medical writers, including Ficino, where they take on the authenticity of a scientific explanation.

In Achilles Tatius' work, we find numerous examples of the eyes' effect. One of the characters of the romance discusses how love has overcome him:

> No sooner did I see her than my fate was sealed — for beauty inflicts a wound sharper than any arrow, finding a passage to the soul through the eyes, for it is the eye which makes a way for the wounds of love. [37]

Later Clinias comments upon the power of the eyes in love and states that seeing the Beloved gives greater pleasure than enjoying her physically:

> And why so? Because the eyes, when encountering each other, receive bodily impressions, as in a looking glass, and

---

[35] *The Greek Romances of Heliodorus, Longus and Achilles Tatius,* trans. R. Smith (London, 1855), pp. 69-70.

[36] Pliny, *Natural History,* trans. H. Rackman (Cambridge and London: Loeb Classical Library, 1940), Book VIII, pp. 57-8: "In Western Ethiopia ... there is an animal called the catoblepas, in other respects of moderate size and inactive with the rest of its limbs, only with a very heavy head which it carries with difficulty — it is always hanging down to the ground; otherwise it is deadly to the human race, as all who see its eyes expire immediately.

The basilisk serpent also has the same power. It is a native of the province of Cyrenaica, not more than twelve inches long and adorned with a bright white marking on the head like a sort of diadem. It routs all snakes with its hiss [...]. It kills bushes not only by its touch but also by its breath, scorches up grass and bursts rocks. Its effect on other animals is disastrous: it is believed that once one was killed with a spear by a man on horseback and the infection rising through the spear killed not only the rider but also the horse."

[37] Achilles Tatius, *The Greek Romances* [...], op. cit., p. 354.

the reflection of beauty glancing into the soul, begets union
even in separation [. . .] the eye is a wondrous vehicle of
love and constant intercourse is most influential in beget-
ting kindly feelings. [38]

Later still, there is an interesting interlude between Melitta and
her lover as they gaze enraptured at each other. Once again, the
description is accompanied by a philosophical and physiological commentary:

> Lovers find their chief delight in gazing upon the beloved;
> and when once this tender passion has taken possession
> of the soul, there is not time or desire for taking food.
> The pleasure conceived by the eyes flows through them
> into the mind, bears along with it the image of the beloved
> and impresses its form upon the mirror of the soul; the
> emanation of beauty darting like secret rays and leaving
> its outline on the love-sick heart. [39]

In a subsequent passage, an interesting connection is established
between beauty as the inspirer of love and the eyes:

> It is in the eyes that beauty has its seat and Thersander
> caught a momentary glimpse of the beauty which (rapid
> as lightning) flashed from hers, and was at once on fire
> with love, and waited spellbound, in hopes of her raising
> them again; but when she continued to gaze upon the
> ground, he said: "Fair maiden, why waste the light of
> the eyes upon the earth, why not look up and let them
> dart fresh light into me?" [40]

The last example of the topos to which we will refer in Greek
literature comes from the fifth or sixth century work by Musaeus
Grammaticus, *Hero and Leander*. Here, Hero's eyes project flaming
arrows into Leander's eyes which inflame him with passionate love.
Once again, beauty is pictured as responsible for the shaft sent out
by the Lady's eyes, and the Beholder's eyes are represented as the
open doorway to his heart:

---

[38] Ibid., p. 360-361.
[39] Ibid., p. 445.
[40] Ibid., p. 464.

Mais toi, malheureux Léandre, dès que tu vis la noble vierge, tu ne souffris pas que ton cœur s'épuisât en silence sous les coups d'aiguillon. Dompté soudain par les flèches de flamme, tu n'admis plus de vivre sans posséder la splendide Héro; le brandon des amours s'attisait à l'éclat de ses yeux, et ton cœur bouillonnait sous l'ardeur d'une flamme invincible. Car la beauté partout célébrée d'une femme irréprochable atteint les mortels d'un trait plus rapide que la flèche ailée. C'est par l'œil que ce trait passe; de l'œil, qui le lance, la beauté glisse et chemine jusqu'au cœur de l'homme. A ce moment, donc, l'admiration, l'audace, l'effroi, le respect le retenait de se laisser prendre. Mais, tandis qu'il admirait cette beauté parfaite, l'amour chassa le respect. Hardiment, poussé par l'amour, que l'audace séduit, il s'approcha doucement et s'arrêta devant la jeune fille. Tout en l'épiant du coin de l'œil, il se mit à lui décocher d'insidieux regards. Par de muets signes de tête, il cherchait à égarer son cœur. [41]

An interesting development here is that once Leander is smitten by the arrows from Hero's eyes, he too adopts the same strategy and in turn casts glances at her in the hope of producing in her heart the same result that has befallen his own.

\* \* \*

From this brief survey, we can see that the representation of the eyes as love's principal agent was a well-established tradition in Greek literature and was often combined with a pseudo-scientific and psychological commentary on the way the eyes were able to exert their influence over the Other. It therefore comes as something of a surprise to find what Ruth Cline has called the "meager representation" [42] of these elements in the classical Latin poets. The eyes are rarely more than passive receivers of love and beauty (although their importance in this regard as certainly stressed). While these poets sometimes represent eyes as being full of flames, it is rare that the flames are projected at others as in the Greek tradition we have been examining. Dart and arrow imagery abounds in Latin amatory literature, but the darts are almost always hurled by Cupid

---

[41] Musaeus, *Héro et Léandre,* trans. Pierre Orsini (Paris, 1968), ll. 86 ff.
[42] Cline, op. cit., p. 276.

himself and are rarely, if ever, associated with the eyes. While the Latin poets do recognise the importance of the eyes in love (as evidenced by the quotation from Propertius at the beginning of this chapter), the eyes are the entrance by which love enters the soul, so that when Propertius writes: "Oculi in amore duces," he really means that the eyes of the Beholder give admittance to love and lead it to the heart. The eyes themselves are neither the aggressors in the love relationship nor are they the initiators of love. As Cline has pointed out,[43] in Ovid we never find the God of Love shooting an arrow through the eye to the heart of the Lover, one of the most important aspects of the topos. Cupid's shaft goes directly into the heart of his victim without passing through the eyes.

In fact, if we wish to follow the continuation of the aggressive-eye topos between Greek and medieval European literature, we need to turn to Arabic literature where the eyes' role in engendering love is a constant theme. Cline remarks: "In the Arabic erotic literature [...] love at first sight is conventional. Also it is largely fatal; that is, an ifrit or jinn may, in the place of Eros, be working his will in bringing the lovers together, or the effect upon the beholder of the sudden sight of a beautiful woman may be so great that the lover is powerless to resist this influence."[44] Cline bases her study of the Arabic continuation of the topos above all on the *Arabian Nights* and the codification of the traditions of love which appeared in Ibn Hazm's *Tawq* or *Dove's Neck-Ring*. However, the topos does appear earlier in Arabic love poetry and needs to be examined not only in the *Arabian Nights,* but also in the amatory and mystical poetry which is contemporary with this remarkable collection of tales. Even before the probable date of their appearance, in the sixth century A. D., we already find that the eyes are represented as lethal weapons which instill love by their glance. In the *Mu'allaqa of Imr Al-Qais,* we read:

---

[43] Ibid., p. 282.

[44] Ibid., p. 279. Dr. Cline also investigates Hebrew and Biblical sources as influences on the development of the theme. However, while these sources are important in the heart/eyes relationship on which her study concentrates, they contribute little to the aggressive presentation of vision we find in the aggressive eye topos.

Your eyes only shed those tears so as to strike and pierce
with those two shafts of theirs the fragments of a ruined
heart. [45]

The poet Bashbar ben Bard (c. 783) warns of the effects of a
beautiful woman's glance:

> The beautiful girl who rivaled the moon
> [...]
> Her eyes, black like those of the gazelle
> Slew her lovers and did not revive them. [46]

This description is echoed in a twelfth century ode to mystical love
by the poet Ibn al-Farid:

> O you with stilled heart!
> Do not look at my beloved;
> Stay free of her black eyes' threat. [47]

In fact, the whole gamut of imagery associated with the eyes as
love's agent is found in the works of this mystical poet. Arberry
has catalogued these images in his study of Arabic poetry:

> *Glances*: The beloved's glances are compared with arrows
> or sword-blades, piercing the lover's heart.
> i) III, 13. Refrain — may I have naught of thee! — and
> reject thou him whose bowels have been mercilessly
> wounded by wide-eyed enchanters.
> ii) V, 4. O thou who aimest, as one who aimeth the
> arrows of his glances from the bow of his curved eyebrows,
> against my bowels to transfix them.
> iii) V, 10. A sword his eyelids draw against my heart,
> and I see the very languor thereof doth whet its blade.
> iv) VI, I. Guard thou thy heart if thou passest by Hajir,
> for the gazelles there dwelling have swords flashing in the
> orbits of their unveiled eyes.
> v) IX, 29. My people know well that I am slain by her
> glances: for in every limb of her she possesses a whetted
> point.

---

[45] A. J. Arberry, *The Seven Odes* (London, 1957), p. 62.
[46] Najib Ullah, *Islamic Literature* (New York, 1963), p. 47.
[47] Ibid., p. 157.

vi) IX, 36.   No eye hath alighted on any trace of me, nor
have those wide eyes left any remaining mark of me in
my passion.

vii) XIII, 26.   The arrow of the clever one of the tribe
pierced me, but missed my vitals; the arrow of your glances
hath scorched my bowels utterly. [48]

These themes were widespread not only in the mystical love poetry
of the period but also in its amatory love verse. The poet Mu'izzi
(c. 1150) uses the same imagery in talking of his Beloved:

Thine eye, by wounding heart, hath made me helpless
Thy tress, by ravishing my soul, hath made me distraught.
If thine eye pierces my heart, 'tis right, for thou art my sweetheart. [49]

Anwari (c. 1190) describes his love in similar fashion, specifically
comparing her glance to an arrow and the eyebrow to the bow
which shoots the arrow. This is proof that this particular image
had no need of the myth of an arrow-shooting Eros to make it
viable:

Her ringlet's tip was leading in chains one thousand hearts.
Against the soul in ambush her looks had loosed their might,
Her amorous glance an arrow, poised on the eyebrows' bow. [50]

The importance of the eye as receptor of love is also mentioned in
the *Dove's Neck-Ring,* although the theme of the eye as aggressor
does not appear. However, the eyes are presented as playing a most
important role in the love experience as they are designated as the
gateway to the soul. When speaking of the signs of love, Ibn Hazm
says:

Love has its symptoms which are detected by the sagacious
man, and by which are guided the intelligent man. The
first of them is the continuous look: indeed, the eye is
the wide open gate of the soul. [51]

---

[48] A. J. Arberry, *Arabic Poetry* (Cambridge, 1965), p. 20.
[49] R. A. Nicholson, *Studies in Islamic Poetry* (Cambridge, 1921), p. 23.
[50] Ibid., p. 29.
[51] Ibn Hazm, *The Risala known as The Dove's Neck-Ring,* trans. A. R. Nykl
(Paris, 1931), p. 15.

When we turn to the *Arabian Nights,* we are confronted with
a multitude of images picturing the eyes as instigators of love. A
few typical examples will suffice to show that the entire range of
eye imagery we have been examining is present: eyes shooting arrows which wound the heart, eyes casting spells, eyebrows as the
bows from which glances are shot:

> Thereupon sat a lady [. . .] with brow beaming brilliancy,
> the dream of philosophy, whose eyes were fraught with
> Babel's gramarye and her eyebrows were arched as for
> archery [. . .] [52]

Or again:

> [. . .] and she shot through all hearts with the magical
> shaft of her eye-babes [. . .] And she clave all hearts with
> the arrows of her eyelashes [. . .] [53]

Or:

> From the fringed curtains of her eyne she shoots shafts
> which at farthest range on mark alight [. . .] [54]

Or later in the "49th Night":

> [. . .] those eyne! What streams of blood they shed! How
> many an arrowy glance those lids of thine have sped. [55]

Or at the conclusion of the work:

> [. . .] for that they had eyes sharper than unsheathed
> swords and the lashes of their eyelids bewitched all
> hearts. [56]

An unusual feature of the transmission and development of the
aggressive eye topos is that it lies dormant in European literature

---

[52] *The Book of the Thousand Nights and a Night,* trans. Richard F. Burton
(Burton Club, no date), vol. 1, p. 85.
[53] Ibid., vol. 1, p. 218.
[54] Ibid., vol. 1, p. 219.
[55] Ibid., vol. 2, p. 200.
[56] Ibid., vol. 10, p. 57.

at this time and only starts to reappear with the Provençal poets. It would seem reasonable to adopt Ruth Cline's conclusion, that, in view of the meager representation of the theme in the classical Latin authors, when it does reappear, Arabic literature seems to be the most likely immediate source. And so we witness the unusual phenomenon of an important commonplace being most probably created and certainly nurtured in early Greek literature and then being transmitted to later European literature, not by way of Latin literature, but most probably through Arabic writers.

When we turn to the Provençal poets of the twelfth century, we find almost a carbon copy of the portrait of the Lady's eyes we have just seen in Arabic literature. The troubadour Peire Vidal describes his mistress in two stanzas of his poem "Tant an ben dig des marques" within the framework of a military metaphor in which the poet is vanquished by the glances of his Beloved:

> Per so m'an Lombart conques,
> Pos m'appellet 'car messier'
> Tals qu'anc no vist nulh arquier
> Tan dreg ni tan prim traisses;
> E.m fier al cor ses falhensa
> Ab un cairel de plazensa,
> Fabregat el foc d'amor,
> Temprat de doussa sabor.

> E l'olh e.l cil negre espes
> E.l nas qu'es en loc d'arbrier,
> Ve.us l'arc de qu'aitals colps fier
> Ab un esgart demanes,
> Don escut no.lh fai garensa:
> E pos a leis platz que.m vensa,
> No m'o tenh a dezonor,
> Si.ls fortz venson li forsor. [57]

---

[57] Peire Vidal, *Les poésies,* ed. and trans. J. Anglade (Paris, 1923), pp. 110-112: "Si les Lombards m'ont conquis, c'est que je fus appelé 'cher messire' par une dame qui frappe plus droit et plus juste que le meilleur archer; elle me frappe au cœur, sans me manquer, avec un agréable trait, forgé au feu d'amor, trompé de douce saveur. Les yeux, les cils noirs et épais, le nez qui est en forme d'arc, voilà l'arc dont elle frappe de tels coups, dès qu'elle vous regarde, qu'aucun bouclier ne peut vous protéger; puisqu'il lui plaît de me vaincre, je ne m'en tiens pas pour déshonoré, si les forts sont vaincus par de plus forts."

It is the Lady's glance which penetrates right to the Lover's heart
and brings him refreshment and joy in Bernard de Ventadour's "En
cossirer et en esmai":

> Negus jois almen no s'eschai,
> can ma domna'm garda ni'm ve,
> que 'l seus bels douz semblans me vai
> al cor, que d'adous' e'm reve [. . .] [58]

In another poem we have an interesting treatment of Plato's theory
of the Lover seeing himself in the mirror of his Beloved's eyes, so
that the Lover becomes another Narcissus:

> Anc non agui de me poder
> ni no fui meus de l'or'en sai
> que'm laisset en sos olhs vezer
> en un miralh que mout me plai.
> Miralhs, pus me mirei en te,
> m'an mort li sospir de preon,
> c'aissi'm perdei com perdet se
> lo bels Narcissus en la fon. [59]

The Greco-Arabic influence is also palpable in mediaeval romances when they deal with love at first sight. In the *Roman
d'Enéas*, for example, Lavinia is wounded by the God of Love as
she contemplates Eneas. At first, the portrayal of the *innamoramento*
appears more Ovidian than Greek. Cupid wounds here by shooting
an arrow directly into her heart:

> Amors l'a de son dart ferue;
> [. . .]
> la saiete li est colee
> des i qu'el cuer soz la mamele. [60]

---

[58] Bernart de Ventadorn, *Chansons d'amour*, ed. Moshé Lazar (Paris, 1966),
p. 216. Translation (Lazar): "Aucune joie n'est comparable à la mienne
lorsque ma dame me regarde et me contemple, car son beau et doux regard
me va droit au cœur, me remplit de douceur et me rassure."

[59] Ibid., p. 180. Translation: "Je n'eus plus pouvoir sur moi-même et je
ne m'appartiens plus dès l'instant où elle me laissa regarder dans ses yeux,
en ce miroir qui me plaît beaucoup. Miroir, depuis que je me suis miré en
toi, les profonds soupirs ont causé ma mort, si bien que je me suis perdu
comme se perdit le beau Narcisse dans la fontaine."

[60] *Le Roman d'Enéas*, ed. Jacques Salverda de Grave (Halle, 1891), ll. 8057
ff., pp. 299-300.

Later, however, this arrow is directly associated with the eye when in lines 8158 ff. Lavinia voices her complaint against love:

> N'avra Amors de mei merci?
> Il me navra en un esguart,
> en l'oil me feri de son dart,
> de celui d'or, ki fait amer;
> tot le me fist el cuer coler.

It is the Beloved's glance (*esguart*) which is ultimately responsible for the wound in her heart.

When we turn to Chrétien de Troyes, we find much more attention devoted to the "esguart" which transmits love, as this theme is often accompanied by the same type of psychological and physiological analysis which we saw in the third century A.D. Greek romances. It is in *Cligès* where we find the most elaborate working of the topos, in the section which deals with the love of Soredamor and Alexandre. Soredamor, previously disdainful of passion, here laments her conquest at the hands of Cupid:

> Oel, vos m'avez traïe;
> Par vos m'a mes cuers anhaïe,
> Qui me soloit estre de foi [...] [61]

When Alexandre finds himself in the same state, he is even more explicit. It is Love who is first blamed but then the role of the eyes is mentioned and a curious debate occurs within Alexandre's mind as to how Love gained entrance to his soul:

> Cest mal me fet Amors avoir.
> [...]
> Nenil qu'il m'a navré si fort
> Que jusqu'au cuer m'a son dart trait,
> Mes ne l'a pas a lui retrait.
> Comant le t'a donc trait el cors,
> Quant la plaie ne pert de fors?
> Ce me diras; savoir le vuel!
> Comant le t'a il tret? Par l'uel.
> Par l'uel? Si ne le t'a crevé?
> A l'uel ne m'a il rien grevé,
> Mes au cuer me grieve formant.

---

[61] Chrétien de Troyes, *Cligés,* ed. A. Micha (Paris, 1957), ll. 469 ff.

Or me di donc reison comant
Li darz est par mi l'uel passez,
Qu'il n'an est bleciez ne quassez.
Se li darz parmi l'uel i antre,
Li cuers por coi s'an dialt el vantre,
Que li ialz aussi ne s'an dialt,
Qui le premier cop an requialt? [62]

The eye also plays an important role in the *Roman de la Rose*. One of Cupid's companions goes by the name of Doux Regard and carries with him "deux arcs turcois," symbolic of the eyebrows. The Ovidian theme of Cupid shooting arrows of gold and lead appears here in the variation that one of the bows belonging to Doux Regard is black and made of knotty wood, while the other is smooth and attractively fashioned. The ugly bow has five arrows representing the antitheses of love ("Orgueil," "Vilenie" etc.), while of the other bow's five arrows, the first is "Beauté." When Cupid attacks the Lover, he uses Doux Regard's weapons and shoots through the Lover's eyes:

Il a tantost pris une floiche,
E quant la corde fu en coche,
Il entesa jusqu'a l'oreille
L'arc qui estoit forz a mervoille,
E tret a moi par tel devise
Que par mi l'ueil m'a ou cuer mise
La saiete par grant roidor. [63]

A tittle later, the author reiterates that: "le fer m'entra par l'œil dans le cœur":

Si que par l'ueil ou cuer m'entra
La saiete qui me navra [64]

When Cupid is instructing Bel Ami in the ways of love, the importance of Doux Regard is once more stressed:

Li tierz biens vient de regarder,
C'est Douz Regart, qui seut tarder

---

[62] Ibid., 1. 658 and ll. 684 ff.
[63] Guillaume de Lorris et Jean de Meun, *Le roman de la rose,* ed. Félix Lecoy (Paris, 1968), ll. 1687 ff.
[64] Ibid., ll. 1741-42.

A ceus qui ont amors loigtienes.
Mes je te lo que tu te tiegnes
Bien pres de li por Douz Regart,
Que ses solaz trop ne te tart;
Car il est mout as amoreux delitables et savoreus
Mout ont au matin bone encontre
Li oil, quant Damedex lor montre
Le saintuaire precieus
De quoi i sont si envieus.
[...]
Car li oil, con droit mesagier,
Tot maintenant au cuer envoient
Noveles de ce que il voient,
Et por la joie covient lors
Que li cuer oblit ses dolors
Et les teniebres ou il ere.
Tot autresi con la lumiere
Les teniebres devant soi chace,
Tot ausi Douz Regarz achace
Les teniebres ou li cuers gist
Qui nuit et jor d'amors languist,
Car li cuers de rien ne se diaut
Quant li oil voient ce qu'il viaut. [65]

The utilisation of the aggressive eye topos by the Provençal poets and the poets of mediaeval romances was emulated in Italy well before the time of Petrarch. Giacomo da Lentini, a poet of the *Scuola siciliana,* shares the same concern as Chrétien de Troyes regarding the manner in which the Beloved's image can enter the Lover's body given the fact that the eyes are so small and the Beloved is, in comparison, so large:

Or come pote si gran donna entrare
per gli oc(c)hi mei, che sì pic(c)ioli sone?
e nel mio core come pote stare,
che 'nentr' esso la porto laonque i'vone?
   (Lo) loco laonde entra già non pare,
ond 'io gran meraviglia me ne dòne;
ma voglio lei a lumera asomigliare,
e gli oc(c)hi mei al vetro ove si póne.
   Lo foco inchiuso, poi passa di fore
lo suo lostrore, sanza far rot(t)ura:
cosi per gli oc(c)hi mi pass'a lo core,

---

[65] Ibid., ll. 2701-12; 2722-34.

> no la persona, ma la sua figura.
> Rinovellare mi voglio d'amore,
> poi porto in segna di tal criatura. [66]

In another sonnet the same poet ascribes supremacy to the eyes in inspiring love:

> Amor è un(o) desio che ven da core
> per abondanza di gran piacimento;
> e li occhi in prima genera(n) l'amor
> e lo core li dà nutricamento. [67]

Pier della Vigna affirms the same primacy for the eyes and uses the familiar dart imagery to convey the penetrating power of a love glance:

> Uno piasente isguardo
> coralmente m'ha feruto,
> und' eo d'amore sentomi infiammato
>    ed è stato uno dardo
> pungent' e si forte acuto
> che mi passao lo core e m'ha 'ntamato. [68]

Stafano Protonotaro da Messina likens the love-inspiring glance of the Beloved to the basilisk's look which brings death to the Beholder:

> Poi che m'appe ligato,
> co li occhi sorrise,
> si ch'a morte mi mise
> como lo badalisco. [69]

Such eye imagery was continued and developed by the poets of the *dolce stil nuovo*. Guido Cavalcanti identifies the Lady's eyes as the home of love and the vantage point from which Cupid shoots his arrows:

> O tu, che porti nelli occhi sovente
> Amor tenendo tre saette in mano [ . . . ] [70]

---

[66] *Poeti del Duecento,* ed. G. Contini (Milano, no date), vol. 2, p. 76.
[67] Ibid., p. 90.
[68] Ibid., p. 123.
[69] Ibid., p. 138.
[70] Ibid., p. 514.

When the Lady's eyes do not shoot arrows, there emanates from them a warm "spirito d'amore":

> Ell mi fere si, quando la sguardo,
> ch' i' sento lo sospir tremar nel core:
>   esce degli occhi suoi, che me [...] ardo,
> un gentiletto spirito d'amore [...] [71]

The "spirito" becomes a "spiritello" in a poem of Lapo Gianni, a "spiritello" which issues forth from the Beloved's eyes:

> D'entr'al tuo cor si mosse un spiritello,
> esci per li occhi e vennem' a ferire
> quando guardai lo tuo viso amoroso [...] [72]

These motifs are encountered again in Dante's poetry. While a great deal of importance is attributed to Beatrice's star-like eyes in the *Divine Comedy,* it is particularly in his *canzoniere* and to a lesser extent in the *Vita nuova* that we find the type of eye imagery we have been examining. Once more the Lady's eyes are the source of Love:

> Ne li occhi porta la mia donna Amore,
> per che si fa gentil ciò ch'ella mira;
> ov' ella passa, ogn'om ver lei si gira,
> e cui saluta fa tremar lo core [...] [73]

The spirit of love flashes from her eyes and inflames the heart of him who beholds her:

> De li occhi suoi, come ch'ella li mova,
> escono spirti d'amore inflammati,
> che feron li occhi a qual che allor la guati,
> e passan sì che 'l cor ciascun retrova [...] [74]

As it is above all to Petrarch and the Italian Petrarchan poets that critics have attributed the aggressive eye topos, the petrarchan examples of it are well known. Accordingly we will only refer to a

---

[71] Ibid., p. 534.
[72] Ibid., p. 577.
[73] Dante, *La vita nuova,* ed. Natalino Sapegno (Florence, 1931), p. 75.
[74] Ibid., p. 72.

small sampling of them to show how the tradition was carried on in Italy after Dante. Archery imagery is used to represent the *innamoramento* in sonnet LXXXVII of the *Rime*:

> Sì tosto come aven che l'arco scocchi,
> buon sagittario di lontan discerne
> qual colpo è da sprezzare, e qual d'averne
> fede ch'al destinato segno tocchi:
>      similemente il colpo de' vostr'occhi,
> donna, sentiste a le mie parti interne
> dritto passar, onde conven ch'eterne
> lagrime per la piaga il cor trabocchi. [75]

Laura's glance is compared to that of Medusa:

> pò quello in me, che nel gran vecchio mauro
> Medusa, quand in selce trasformollo; [76]

And battle imagery is used to describe the eyes' incapacity to repel the assault of love in sonnet II:

> Era la mia virtute al cor ristretta
> per far ivi e negli occhi sue difese,
> quando 'l colpo mortal là giú discese,
> ove solea spuntarsi ogni saetta. [77]

Petrarch's contemporary, Boccaccio, used similar imagery in his romance, *Amorous Fiammetta,* to describe the first time Fiammetta fell in love:

> Ma infra l'altre volte che io, non guardandomi dalli amorosi lacciuoli, il mirai, tenendo alquanto più fermi che l'usato ne'suoi li occhi miei [...] perchè non altrimenti il fuoco sè stesso d'una parte in un'altra balestra, che una luce, per un raggio sottilissimo trascorrendo, da' suoi par-

---

[75] Petrarca, *Canzoniere,* ed. G. Contini (Torino, 1964), Sonnet LXXXVII, ll. 1-8, p. 120.
  Cf. Lucian's Portraits where Lycinus says: "Oui [...] ce qu'on éprouvait jadis à la vue de la Gorgone, je viens de l'éprouver tout à l'heure en voyant une belle femme. Peu s'en faut que je n'aie été pétrifié comme dans la Fable [...]." Lucian, *Œuvres complètes,* trans. E. Talbot (Paris, 1866), vol. 2, p. 1.
[76] Petrarca, Sonnet CXCVII, ll. 5-6, p. 253.
[77] Ibid., Sonnet II, ll. 5-8, p. 4.

ordrrer.

tendosi, percosse nelle occhi miei, nè in quelli contenta rimase, anzi, non so per quali occulte vie, subitamente al cuore penetrando, ne gìo. Il quale, nel subito avvenimento di quella temendo, rivocate a se le forze esteriori, me pallida e quasi tutta freddissima lasciò; [. . .] Questo fu quel giorno, nel quale io prima, di libera donna, divenni miserissima serva: questo fu quel giorno, nel quale io prima amore, non mai prima da me cognosciuto, conobbi: questo fu quel giorno, nel quale premieramente li venerei veleni contaminarono il puro et casto petto. [78]

In France in the final years of the Gothic era, Charles d'Orléans was also warning against the insidious power of the eyes to engender love. In one of his poems, it is the allegorical figure *Beauté* who wounds him with a dart sent through his eyes:

Mes yeulx prindrent fort à la regarder,
Plus longuement ne les en peu garder.
Quant Beauté vit que je la regardoye,
Tost par mes yeulx un dard au cœur m'envoye. [79]

In yet another he enjoins his lady to look elsewhere, as he is unable to resist the powerful onslaught of her gaze:

Vueilliez voz yeulx emprisonner,
Et sur moy plus ne les giettés;
Car quant vous plaist me regarder
Par Dieu, Belle vous me tués [. . .] [80]

By the end of the Middle Ages then, and in the early Renaissance, the topos of the eye as aggressor/receptor in love was firmly established in amatory literature. With the arrival of the Renaissance proper, this literary tradition was carried on and expanded, thanks in part to the renewal of interest in Plato and the almost overwhelming influence exerted by neo-platonism and its prophet Ficino. The role of the eyes in love became a serious preoccupation of neo-platonic thinkers and writers, as the nature of love itself

[78] Boccaccio, *Fiammetta,* ed. G. Gigli (Strasburg: Biblioteca Italiana, no date), pp. 28-30.
[79] Charles d'Orléans, *Poésies complètes,* ed. Charles Héricault (Paris, no date), vol. 1, p. 7.
[80] Ibid., p. 15.

became central to their philosophising. The original platonic theory of vision was embellished with examples from the writings of the numerous authors who had contributed to the continuation and spread of the aggressive eye topos. This tradition was fostered not only by the Italian Petrarchan poets such as Bembo and Serafino, but also by Ficino, Leone Ebreo and by such savants as the Parisian physician Jacques Ferrand. We find developments of it even in a work like Robert Burton's *Anatomy of Melancholy*. The prestige and importance the topos acquired is evidenced in the famous passage from Ficino's commentary on Plato's *Symposium*. In the fourth chapter of the *Oratio septima,* the transmission of love by the eyes is described in great pseudo-scientific detail. After explaining how during youth the blood is light, clear and warm, Ficino then goes on to expound how, because of its lightness, it can in fact mingle with the emanations from the eyes (we are back to the efflux theory of vision) and be transmitted to the object or person being looked at:

> Or comme cette vapeur des esprits est tirée du sang, ainsi elle lance elle-même des rayons de même nature que lui à travers les yeux qui sont comme des fenêtres vitrées. De même, comme le soleil qui est le cœur du monde répand sa lumière en suivant sa course et par cette lumière communique ses vertus aux régions inférieures, ainsi le cœur de notre corps, en agitant le sang qui l'entoure d'une sorte de mouvement perpétuel répand dans tout le corps les esprits qu'il en tire, et par ces esprits transmet des étincelles de lumière à travers tous les membres et surtout à travers les yeux [...]
>
> D'autre part que le rayon de lumière émis par les yeux entraîne avec lui la vapeur de l'esprit et que cette vapeur entraîne le sang, nous en avons une preuve dans le fait que des yeux chassieux et rouges communiquent par l'emission de leurs rayons leur propre maladie aux yeux de ceux qui les regardent. Ce qui montre bien et que ce rayon porte jusqu'à celui qu'il regarde et qu'avec ce rayon sort une vapeur de sang corrompu dont la contagion affecte l'œil de l'observateur. Aristote écrit qu'à l'époque de leurs règles, les femmes tachent souvent leur miroir de gouttes de sang. Je pense que la raison de ce phénomène est que l'esprit, qui est une vapeur de sang, est sans doute un sang si léger qu'il échappe à la vue, mais qu'en devenant

plus épais sur la surface d'un miroir il devient clairement perceptible. [81]

Ficino continues his explanation of this phenomenon and then turns to the analogy of the breath which is usually invisible but which condenses on a mirror when it meets its surface. If an invisible vapour from the mouth behaves in this way, why should we be surprised that the eyes can perform in similar fashion?

> Dans ces conditions, qu'y a-t-il d'étonnant qu'un œil ouvert et fixé sur quelqu'un lance les traits de ses rayons dans les yeux de la personne qui est proche de lui et qu'avec ces traits, qui sont les véhicules des esprits, il dirige vers elle la vapeur sanguine que nous appelons esprit? [82]

Ficino then retraces the itinerary accomplished by the eye-beam as it carries the "venom" of love to the heart of its victim:

> De là le trait empoisonné traverse les yeux et comme il vient du cœur de celui qui frappe, il recherche, la poitrine de celui qu'il atteint, comme sa propre demeure. Là il blesse le cœur, se brise sur son sommet qui est plus dur et redevient du sang. Mais ce sang étranger empoisonne celui de l'homme blessé, parce qu'il n'est pas de même nature que lui. Or, un sang empoisonné est malade. [83]

Ficino closes this paragraph with a lament:

> Toute la cause et l'origine de ma douleur présente et en même temps mon vrai remède et mon unique salut, c'est sûrement toi, car tes yeux par mes yeux ont pénétré jusqu'au fond de mon cœur, et ont allumé au fond de moi-même un feu ardent. Aie donc pitié de ta victime.

He then goes on to describe, in a free interpretation of Plato's *Phaedrus,* the fascination which occurred between Phaedrus and Lysias:

---

[81] Marsile Ficin, *Commentaire sur le Banquet de Platon,* ed. and trans. Raymond Marcel (Paris, 1956), pp. 246 ff.
[82] Ibid.
[83] Ibid.

Lysias reste bouche bée devant le visage de Phèdre. Phèdre
lance dans les yeux de Lysias les étincelles de ses yeux, et
en même temps que ces étincelles, lui transmet aussi ses
esprits. [84]

In 1536, the platonising Leone Ebreo (or Leo Hebraeus as he
was sometimes called) in his *Dialoghi d'Amore,* elaborates on the
theory that love is like a poison lodged firmly in the physiological
workings of the Lover's body. In speaking of the effect of her
beauty on him, Filone tells Sofia that she is poisonous to him, to
which she tartly replies:

> S: Come velenosa?
> F: Velenosa di tal veleno, che manco se li truova remedio
> che a niuno de' corporali toschi: ché, cosi come il veleno
> va dritto al cuore e di li non si parte fin che abbi consumati
> tutti i spiriti, quali gli vanno dietro, e levando i polsi e
> infrigidando gli estremi leva totalmente la vita, se qualche
> remedio esteriore non se gli approssima, cosi l'immagine
> tua è dentro de la mia mente et di li mai si parte, attaendo
> a sé tutte le virtú e spiriti, e con quelli insieme la vita
> totalmente leverebbe, se non che tua persona esistente di
> fuora mi recupera gli espiriti e sentimenti, levandoli di mano
> la prenda per intertenermi la vita. [85]

This answer raises another problem, for love has been characterised
as divine and Sofia cannot understand how her beauty, which is
divine, can also instill poison into Filone's heart. What transforms
it, Filone tells her, is insatiable desire:

> La tua bellezza in forma più divina che umana a me si
> rappresenta; ma per essere sempre accompagnata d'un pon-
> gitivo e insaziabile desiderio, si converte di dentro in uno
> pernizioso e molto furioso veleno, si che quanto tua bellez-
> za è più eccessiva, tanto produce in me più rabbioso e
> velenoso disio. [86]

Such critical scientific and philosophical discussion concerning the
role of vision in love, together with the long history of the aggres-

---

[84] Ibid.
[85] Leone Ebreo, *Dialoghi d'Amore,* ed. Santiago Caramella (Bari, 1929),
p. 198.
[86] Ibid., pp. 198-99.

sive eye topos and the fact that it had been enthusiastically adopted
by Dante, Petrarch and Boccaccio, mean that we find frequent
examples of its use in the High and Late Italian Renaissance. Ariosto
in his famous and highly influential portrait of Alcyna, devotes most
of a stanza to describing the power of her eyes, which are represented as Cupid's lair:

> Sotto duo negri e sottilissimi archi
> Son duo negri occhi, anzi duo chiari soli,
> Pietosi a riguardare, a mover parchi;
> Intorno cui par ch'Amor scherzi e voli,
> E ch'indi tutta la faretra scarchi
> E che visibilmente i cori involi [ . . . ] [87]

In the subsequent enchantment of Roger, it is curious that after
having attributed so much importance to Alcyna's eyes, Ariosto
makes no use of them in describing Roger's falling in love. However, that Ariosto was fully conscious of the importance of the
theme even if he did not fully exploit it in *Orlando furioso* is
clearly evident in his treatment of love in his sonnets, particularly
in Sonnet VI where he uses the image of the eyebrow as bow and
the glance as the arrow which wounds the Lover:

> La rete fu di queste fila d'oro,
> In che il mio pensier vago intricò l'ale
> E queste ciglia l'arco, e 'l guardo strale
> E 'l feritor questi begli occhi foro. [88]

The eye topos is also frequently used in the Petrarchan poets. In a
sonnet in which the Lover is compared to a young deer wounded
by the Beloved (a sonnet which proved particularly popular in the
French Renaissance and was successfully imitated by Ronsard, among
others), Bembo describes the Lady's eyes as a huntress casting their
arrows at the Lover:

> Ne teme di saetta o d'altro inganno;
> Se non quand' ella è colta in mezzo 'l fianco,
> Da buon arcier che di nascosto scocchi.

[87] Ariosto, *Orlando furioso,* ed. S. Debenedetti (Bari, 1928), Book 7,
stanza 12.
[88] Ariosto, *Opere,* ed. A. Racheli (Trieste, 1857), Sonnet VI.

> Tal io senza temer vicino affanno
> Mossi Donna quel dì; che bei vostr'occhi
> Me 'mpiagar lasso tutto 'l lato manco. [89]

Bembo also pictures the Lady's eyes as Cupid's abode (or at least as the vantage point from which he shoots his arrows):

> Occhi leggiadri, onde sovente Amore
> Move lo stral, che la mia vita impiaga [. . .] [90]

And like Lucian, he compares his Beloved to Medusa, thus attesting to the frightening power of her glance:

> Medusa s'egli è ver, che tu di noi
> Facevi pietra, assai fosti men dura
> Di tal, che m'arde, strugge, agghiaccia, e' ndura. [91]

This comparison is also used by Serafino in his Sonnet XI:

> Quel nimico mortal de la natura
> Che ardí ferir piú volté omini e dei
> In marmo è qui converso da costei;
> Che col dolce mirar gli animi fura
> Ferir la volse un dí senza aver aura
> A quelli ardenti sguardi medusei,
> Et a questi alti monti, che per lei
> D'omini son conversi in pietra dura. [92]

And Bembo in *Gli Asolani* also attests, even though somewhat disparagingly, to the importance bestowed upon the eyes as he uses archery image to refer to his Lady:

> Chi non sa fare incontanente quella, che esso ama, saettatrice; fingendo che gli occhi suoi ferischano di pungentissime saette? [93]

The eyes also play an important role in Castiglione's portrayal of love in the *Courtier* and here the influence of Ficino is manifest

---

[89] Pietro Bembo, *Opere, Vol. 2 Rime* (Venezia, 1729).
[90] Bembo, Sonnet XIII.
[91] Bembo, Sonnet LXXII.
[92] Serafino Aquilano Cimino, *Le Rime* (Bologna, 1894), Sonnet XI.
[93] Bembo, *Gli Asolani* (Vinegia, 1515), p. 54 v.

in the physiological description of the passage of love through the Lover's body. In order to reveal his love to his Lady, the Courtier is advised to make full use of the power of his eyes:

> [. . .] far che gli occhi siano que' fidi messaggeri, che portino l'ambasciate del core; perché spesso con maggior efficacia mostran quello che dentro vi è di passione, che la lingua propria . . . di modo che non solamente scoprono i pensieri, ma spesso accendono amore nel cor della persona amata; perché que' vivi spirti che escono per gli occhi, per esser generati presso al core, entrando ancor negli occhi, dove sono indrizzati come saetta al segno, naturalmente penetrano al core come a sua stanza ed ivi si confondono con quegli altri spirti e, con quella sottilissima natura di sangue che hanno seco, infettano il sangue vicino al core, dove son pervenuti, e lo riscaldono e fannolo a sé simile ed atto a ricevere la impression di quella imagine che seco hanno portata; onde a poco a poco andando e ritornando questi messaggeri la via per gli occhi al core e riportando l'esca e 'l focile di bellezza e di grazia, accendono col vento del desiderio quel foco che tanto arde e mai non finisce di consumare, perché sempre gli apportano materia di speranza per nutrirlo. Però ben dir si po che gli occhi siano guida in amore [. . .] [94]

Castiglione concludes this description of the effect of the eyes by using the military metaphor so frequently associated with their activity. For good measure he also includes the image of the eyes-as-bewitchers, and in so doing manages to include all the principal aspects of the aggressive eye topos in this passage:

> Gli occhi adunque stanno nascosi come alla guerra soldati insidiatori in agguato; e se la forma di tutto 'l corpo è bella e ben composta, tira a sé ed alletta chi da lontan la mira, fin a tanto che s'accosti; e subito che è vicino, gli occhi saetanno ed affaturano come venefici; e massimamente quando per dritta linea mandano i raggi suoi negli occhi della cosa amata in tempo che essi facciano il medesimo; perché i spiriti s'incontrano ed in quel dolce intoppo l'un piglia la qualità dell'altro, come si vede d'un occhio infermo che guardando fisamente in un sano gli dà la sua infirmità [. . .] [95]

---

[94] B. Castiglione, *Il Cortegiano,* ed. Bruno Maier (Torino, 1955), pp. 429-430.
  [95] Ibid., p. 430.

As it is not our purpose in this introductory survey of the aggressive eye topos to give a complete catalogue of its use in the Italian Renaissance but rather to provide a brief general history as a background to its use by the early French Renaissance poets, we will not trace its exploitation beyond the works of Ariosto and Castiglione. However, as a conclusion to this section and as further evidence that the eyes' role in love was an important preoccupation throughout the Renaissance, we will now refer to two theoretical works written towards the end of the period. That interest in the functioning of the eyes in love did not wane, but if anything increased at this time can be seen from the fact that we find ourselves in the presence of extremely detailed accounts of the eyes' workings, notwithstanding the fact that previous authors like Ficino and Castiglione had already delved deeply into these matters. The descriptions of the role of the eyes we are about to read will provide both a useful summary of the principal details of the topos and stress once more its importance in both the thought and literature of the whole Renaissance period.

The first work was written by a Parisian doctor, Jacques Ferrand and entitled *De la maladie d'Amour*. It first appeared in 1612, was re-edited (and probably expanded)[96] in 1623 and was popular enough and considered important enough to have been translated into English in 1640 under the title *Erotomania*. This very complex treatise describes the nature, symptoms, course and cure of love, and although written by a physician, it uses as authority for its explanations not only medical and scientific writers, but literary and philosophical authors as well. Very early in his work, we already find an exposition of the love as poison theory we have seen in Ficino and Ebreo:

> Ces accidens ont occasioné plusieurs de croire, qu'Amour estoit un venin, qui s'engendroit dans nos corps, ou s'y glissoit par la veüe, ou bien estoit causé par des medicamens qu'ils appelloient philtres [...] qui esgaroient le jugement, consommoient le bon sang [...][97]

Later Ferrand affirms the importance of the eyes in the birth of love by referring both to Aristotle and Ficino:

---

[96] I have been unable to procure a copy of the 1612 edition to verify this.
[97] Jacques Ferrand, *De la maladie d'Amour* (Paris, 1623), p. 10.

> Il semble, dict Aristote en ses Ethiques, que le principe
> de toute sorte d'Amour, et d'amitié, soit le plaisir qu'on
> prend par la veue, à raison dequoy le poëte Properce ap-
> polle les yeux les conducteurs et guides de l'amour [...]
> Aussi sont-ils vrayment les fenestres par lesquelles Amour
> entre dans nous, pour attaquer le cerveau, citadelle de
> Pallas, et les conduits par lesquels il s'escoule et glisse,
> dans nos entrailles, comme prouvent doctement et copieu-
> sement Marsile Ficin et Fr. Valeriola en ses Observations
> Medicales, ce qu'ils semblent avoir appris de l'ancien Musée
> [...] en son Hymne des fameux amants Ero et Leander
> [...] [98]

Ferrand continues, evoking the arrow motif:

> L'excellente beauté, dit ce Poëte de la dame, qui est sans
> contredit parfaictement belle, blesse le cœur par l'œil plus
> viste, que la sagette empennée, et des yeux se darde et
> glisse aux entrailles, où il cause un ulcere malin et cacoëthe
> [...] [99]

Ferrand is one of the sources cited by Robert Burton in his
curious encyclopaedia of *melancolia, The Anatomy of Melancholy,*
which appeared in 1621. In his discussion of this psychological
state which exercised such fascination over the late Renaissance
mind, Burton discusses love, for as he says:

> Love is a species of melancholy, and a necessary part of
> this my treatise [...] [100]

Burton expounds the causes of love, starting with the remotest
which he considers to be the stars, and then concentrating on the
most frequent cause, the sight of the Beloved's beauty:

> But the most familiar and usual cause of Love is that which
> comes by sight, which conveys those admirable rays of
> beauty and pleasing graces to the heart. Plotinus derives
> love from sight [...]. The eyes are the harbingers of love
> and the first step of love is sight [...] they as two sluices

---

[98] Ibid., p. 16.
[99] Ibid., p. 17.
[100] Robert Burton, *The Anatomy of Melancholy,* ed. F. Dell and P. Jordan-
Smith (London, 1931), pp. 611-612.

let in the influence of that divine, powerful, soulravishing,
and captivating beauty, which, as one saith (Achilles Tatius)
is sharper than any dart or needle, wounds deeper into the
heart and opens a gap through our eyes to that lovely
wound which pierceth the soul itself [. . .] [101]

However the eyes are not simply the open gates which allow admittance to the onslaught of love, they are also the aggressors, depending on whether they belong to the Lover or the Beloved:

> [. . .] the question is how and by what means Beauty
> produceth this effect? By sight: the Eye betrays the soul
> and is both Active and Passive in this business; it wounds
> and is wounded, is an especial cause and instrument, both
> in the subject and in the object. As tears, it begins in the
> eyes, descends to the breast, it conveys these beauteous
> rays, as I have said, to the heart [. . .] [102]

Ferrand had the eyebeams descending first to the entrails, [103] but
the basic itinerary is the same and provides an interesting example
of the way in which knowledge was transmitted from author to
author in the Renaissance. Burton later quotes Ficino extensively:

> The manner of the fascination, as Ficino declares it is this:
> Mortal men are then especially bewitched, when as by often
> gazing one on the other, they direct sight to sight, join
> eye to eye, and so drink and suck in love between them:
> for the beginning of this is the Eye [. . .]. The rays, as
> some think, sent from the eyes carry certain spiritual
> vapours with them, and so infect the other [. . .]. Ficino
> proves it from blear-eyes, that by sight alone, make others
> blear-eyed: and it is more than manifest that the vapour
> of the corrupt blood doth get in together with the rays
> and so by the contagion the spectators' eyes are infected.
> Other arguments there are of a Basilisk, that kills afar off
> by sight [. . .] [104]

---

[101] Ibid., p. 665.

[102] Ibid., p. 674.

[103] It is interesting that the English version of Ferrand's work (which
appeared in 1640) translates the word "entrailles" as "liver," which was considered by Renaissance medicine to be the seat of desire.

[104] Burton, pp. 681-682.

And a military metaphor is associated with the action of the eyes
in this section together with a final acknowledgement to Ficino:

> [...] we speak of wandering, wanton, adulterous eyes,
> which, as he saith, lie still in wait, as so many soldiers,
> and when they spy an innocent spectator fixed on them,
> shoot him through and presently bewitch him [...]. Hence
> you may perceive how easily and how quickly we may be
> taken in love since at the twinkling of an eye, Phaedrus'
> spirits may so perniciously infect Lysias' blood [...] [105]

We have here all the principal features of the eyes' participation
in the love experience. The eyes play a double role. In the Lover
they become a kind of Achilles' heel, the traitors which allow admittance to the enemy and are the cause of the soul's defeat at the
hands of love. In the Beloved the eyes are aggressors, violating
the Lover's eyes, darting arrows, swords or shafts which transmit
love's influence to the Other. So it is that the aggressive eyes of
the Beloved are seen as Cupid's vantage point, and the eyebeams
transmitting love (but rarely receiving it in return) are often seen
as his arrows, while the Beloved's eyebrows are assimilated to his
bow (or vice versa). The eye beams are also seen as agents of infection, in that their penetration into the Lover's body through his
or her eyes is likened to a venom which poisons the heart and soul
of the Lover. Thus the Beloved's glance is often compared to the
Medusa of Greek mythology or to the legendary basilisk.

What is particularly interesting about this representation of the
role played by the eyes in love is not simply its popularity and
frequency, nor the many variations to which it is susceptible, but
the fact that it is one of the few literary topoi to be based on or
at least supported by philosophical and scientific belief. In this
respect it is perhaps misleading (although convenient) to refer to
it as a pure image, when it is, partly at least, also an expression
of an erroneous but firmly held physiological theory. That it was
also an economical and effective way of describing the power and
suddenness of passion and that it did full justice to the importance
of the eyes in the perception of the outside world and in the ac-

---

[105] Ibid., p. 682.

THE EYES' ROLE IN LOVE LITERATURE

quiring of knowledge, help explain its prevalence and popularity. Coming as they do at the end of a long line of practitioners of the aggressive eye topos, the writers of the Renaissance consider it to be both an accurate description and an appropriate image of the birth of love in the human soul.

# Chapter II

# EYE IMAGERY IN THE POETRY OF DU GUILLET, LABÉ, MAGNY AND TYARD

Doulx de ces yeux le traict qui me foudroye ... [1]

THE AGGRESSIVE eye topos, together with its related clusters of images, is one of the most enthusiastically "imitated" [2] themes in French amatory verse of the sixteenth century. This is particularly true in the poetry of the so-called *Ecole lyonnaise,* [3] "so-called" because it is a loosely knit group of poets with a common intellectual background and shared literary interests and aspirations, but has no "manifesto" nor any clearly delineated poetic programme. Since its most prominent poet, Maurice Scève, was never in any real sense its leader and since no-one troubled to catalogue its official members, as did Ronsard for the *Pléiade,* it therefore becomes a matter of interpretation to decide who should be included in this particular poetic constellation. Scève, Pernette Du Guillet and Louise Labé unquestionably form its nucleus and to this trinity we should add Olivier de Magny and Pontus de Tyard, even though Ronsard bestowed membership in the *Pléiade* upon him. Both Magny and Tyard spent an important part of their lives in Lyons and were in

---

[1] Pontus de Tyard, *Les Erreurs amoureuses,* ed. John A. McClelland (Geneva: Droz, 1967), Sonnet XXX, # 40 (McClelland's numbering), p. 137.

[2] In the French Renaissance sense of literary imitation.

[3] Lyons, situated far from the restricting and reactionary atmosphere of Paris and the Sorbonne, was of course one of the focal points of the French Renaissance. By reason of its strategic geographical position, its extensive commercial enterprises and its importance as a centre of printing, Lyons, with its own Italian colony, was very much attuned to the cultural wind blowing westward across the Alps.

close association with the literary circle which gravitated around Labé and Scève. Fortunately, we do not have to decide, in the context of this study, whether Jacques Peletier Du Mans should be added to their number, since his poetry offers no important examples of the type of eye imagery which we propose to examine. As for Clément Marot who is sometimes associated with the group, his itinerant career made his relationship with Lyons too tenuous for us to include him in spite of his connections with Louise Labé's *salon*. [4] In any case, Marot rarely uses the aggressive eye topos in his love poetry and when he does, it is entirely conventional and is in no way central to his presentation of the *innamoramento*. [5]

Our investigation will bear on those poets of the *Ecole lyonnaise* whose work demonstrates a consistent use of eye imagery in the portrayal of the love experience. We will examine the verse of Du Guillet, Labé, Magny and Tyard, since they are the most frequent practitioners of the aggressive eye topos. As for Maurice Scève, his poetry is so rich in eye imagery that we must reserve a whole chapter for a study of his work.

## Pernette Du Guillet

It is perhaps surprising that Pernette Du Guillet, whose close ties to Maurice Scève have been stressed on many occasions and whose work is often seen as forming a dialogue with Scève's *Délie*, [6] uses the aggressive eye topos relatively infrequently, a characteristic which sets her in sharp contrast to her *Jour*, Scève. The type of specific eye imagery we traced back to Ancient Greek literature is comparatively rare in her *Rymes*, and yet the eyes and the act of seeing are presented as important contributors to love in her poems. While in her epigrammes she makes no explicit use of the aggres-

---

[4] See G. Guillot, *Louise Labé* (Paris: Seghers, 1962), p. 36.

[5] The most noteworthy example we have found in his works — and it is far from noteworthy when compared with the use of eye imagery by other poets of his time — comes from his *Epigrammes* (CXXXVI: "Il salue Anne"), where he gives a passing nod to the topos: "...Dieu Gard le Cueur sus qui sont appuyez / Tous mes desirs. Dieu gard l'Oeil tant adestre / Là où Amour a ses Traictz estuyez; / Dieu gard sans qui gardé je ne puis estre!" in Clément Marot, *Les Epigrammes,* ed. C. A. Mayer (London, 1970), p. 202. The eyes play a minor role elsewhere in his love poetry.

[6] Jacqueline Risset's *Délie ou l'anagramme du désir* (Rome: Mario Bulzini, 1971) is only the latest in a series of works to claim this.

sive topos or its subsidiary images (with one exception which we will examine in due course), she does express her relationship with her Beloved in terms of light and darkness, night and day, in short with images which rely directly upon the exercise of vision. If her first epigramme contains no reference to the eyes or the act of looking (the verb *contempler* is used in the closing line but it is related to the imagination and its contemplation of the spiritual qualities of the Beloved), the following poem compares the Beloved's entrance into the Lover's life to the appearance of the dawn which dispels the blackness of night. Her state before she knew love was one of unremitting darkness, a kind of primeval chaos reminiscent of Earth before the Spirit of God moved upon the face of the waters:

> La nuict estoit pour moy si tresobscure
> Que Terre, et Ciel elle m'obscure issoit [7]

The symbolic nature of the night is immediately suggested by the juxtaposition of *Terre* and *Ciel,* which implies both earthly and cosmic blindness, just as the intensity of the darkness is underlined by the echo of the lexeme *obscur* in the rhyme words of these two lines. Although they do not themselves rhyme, they do constitute in a particularly forceful example of polyptoton a kind of sub-rhyme based on their common etymology and their phonetic similarity, all of which serves to bind the two lines into a closely knit unit. That the night is indeed a figurative night is confirmed in the next two lines when the introduction of natural light into the poem's imagery is unable to dispel the all-pervading darkness which hangs like a pall over the poem's speaker. [8] Not even the arrival of *Midy,* normally the moment of daylight's maximum intensity, has the power to change her state and to lighten her darkness:

> Tant qu'à Midy de discerner figure
> N'avois pouvoir — qui fort me marrissoit:
>> (Ll. 3-4)

---

[7] Pernette Du Guillet, *Rymes,* ed. Victor E. Graham (Geneva: Droz, 1968), Epigramme II, p. 9.

[8] We shall use the terms Speaker, Persona and Lover interchangeably to refer to the *je parlant* of the poem. The term Beloved will designate the person who is the love object in the poetry we will be examining.

The second and longest part of the dizain (ll. 5-10) opens with
the verb *voir* used actively with the Speaker as subject and introduces a dawn (*L'aulbe*) [9] which is not a literal, but a metaphorical
one since it immediately accomplishes what the *Midy* of line 3 was
unable to do:

> Mais quand je vis que l'aulbe apparoissoit
> En couleurs mille et diverse, et seraine,
> Je me trouvay de liesse si pleine
> (Voyant desjà la clarté à la ronde)
> Que commençay louer à voix haultaine
> Celuy qui feit pour moy ce Jour au Monde.

The Cimmerian blackness of the initial quatrain is forever banished
by this new, more powerful source of light which transforms the
original monochromatic and melancholic decor into one of colour
and joy. The eye brings love, light and happiness into the darkness
of the Speaker's soul and the metaphoric connotation of the dawn
becomes quite explicit at the end of the poem when the Beloved
is identified as *ce Jour,* the means by which the Speaker's darkness
was finally dissipated. The spiritual and religious aspects of this
unusual (for Renaissance poetry) *innamoramento* are stressed not
only by the implicit parallels between the epigramme and the Creation story but also by the Speaker's hymn of praise at the end of
the poem. Thanks to the deliberate ambiguity of the last line, it is
unclear whether the *Celuy* referred to is God the Creator of the
*Jour* who is in fact the Beloved, or whether *Celuy* is the Beloved
himself whose god-like presence brings light to the world. In either
case the association between the Beloved and the divine is evident,
as is the relationship between sight and beginning of love, which
here by means of the powerful chiaroscuro imagery becomes an
intensely spiritual experience.

It is true however that this use of the act of seeing by Du
Guillet does not correspond precisely to the scenario of the aggressive eye topos. It might seem at first that, having carefully delineated the scope of the eye imagery we propose to consider, we have
now broadened our discussion to include images of light and dark-

---

[9] It is interesting that *aulbe* (from *alba* meaning white) is used rather
than *aurore,* in order to intensify the relationship of the dawn with light.

ness, thus expanding our subject almost infinitely. And yet the type of chiaroscuro imagery Du Guillet uses here does bear a definite relationship to the eye as a source of love. It is not just because it is the eye which perceives light or its lack that we feel justified in examining her light/darkness imagery, but because there is a special relationship implied here between the Beloved and the eyes (both his and hers). The Beloved is in fact a light-bearer, the sun of the speaker's poetic universe, and as such projects life and light-giving rays into the *nuict tresobscure* of the loveless microcosm. The sun was considered, in the animistic view of the universe which still persisted even during the Renaissance, to be the eye of the macrocosm, just as the eye was considered to be the "sun" of the microcosm. As Leone Ebreo explains it in his *Dialoghi:*

> *Filone:* Adunque cosí come ne l'uomo (che è piccol mondo) l'occhio, fra tutte le sue parti corporee, è come l'intelletto fra tutte le virtú de l'anima, simulacro e seguace di quella, cosí nel gran mondo il sole fra tutti i corporali è come l'intelletto divino fra tutti gli spirituali suo simulacro e suo vero seguace ... E quel ch'io voglio mostrarti è che l'occhio non solamente vede, ma ancora prima illumina ciò che vede; si che consequentemente non credere solo che il sole illumini senza che esso veda, che di tutti i sensi nel cielo solamente quelle del viso si stima che vi sia, molto piú perfettamente che ne l'uomo né in alto animale.
> *Sofia:* Come! i cieli veggono come noi?
> *Filone:* Meglio di noi.
> *Sofia:* Hanno occhi?
> *Filone:* E quali miglior occhi che 'l sole e le stelle ... Questi occhi celesti tanto quanto illuminano tant veggono, e mediante il viso comprendono e conoscono tutte le cose del mondo corporeo e le mutazioni loro. [10]

Du Guillet pursues this initial identification of the Beloved with the sun in subsequent epigrammes. Epigramme IV compares him to Apollo:

> Esprit celeste, et des Dieux transformé
> En corps mortel transmis en ce bas Monde,

----
[10] Leone Ebreo, *Dialoghi d'amore,* ed. Santino Caramella (Bari, 1929), pp. 184-186.

A Apollo peulx estre conformé
Pour la vertu, dont es la source [...]

While the comparison is meant above all as an encomium to his virtue, the choice of Apollo is significant, as this not only suggests the Beloved's poetic skill but also his association with the Sungod, who brings light to the world each day. In fact, the Beloved becomes not only a source of light, a second sun more powerful and more effective in the Lover's universe than the sun of nature, but in a sense her eyes also. This is apparent in Epigramme VIII, where a clearcut distinction is made between natural light and the metaphorical light of love, dispensed by the Beloved. Once again he is qualified by the substantive *Jour* which brings the metaphor of Epigramme II ("feit mon Jour") to its ultimate conclusion: the total identification of the Beloved with light and therefore with the sun.

> Ja n'est besoing que plus je me soucie
> Si le jour fault, ou que vienne la nuict,
> Nuict hyvernale, et sans Lune obscurcie:
> Car tout cela certes riens ne me nuit,
> Puis que mon Jour par clarté adoulcie
> M'esclaire toute, et tant, qu'à la mynuict
> En mon esprit me faict appercevoir
> Ce que mes yeulx ne sceurent oncques veoir.

Here the same antagonism between light and darkness present in the chiaroscuro of Epigramme II is even more fully exploited and the clash between natural darkness and the spiritual illumination produced by the Beloved is even more evident. Just as night (*nuict*) is linguistically and grammatically cancelled out by the word-play in line 4 ("...riens ne me nuit"), so the Beloved's light is more than sufficient to conquer any physical or spiritual darkness the Lover may encounter, as she is able to perceive with the eyes of the spirit what her physical eyes were incapable of revealing to her. Even in the most intense darkness possible (a dark, moonless, winter night at "la mynuict," a thematic counterpoint to the *Midy* of Epigramme II), the Beloved, sun and eye of the Lover's soul, illuminates everything, and by making available a sympathetic medium, namely light, enables the Lover's eyes to pierce the darkness of a loveless world.

The relationship between the Lover and her Beloved is further clarified in Chanson IX which is entirely constructed upon the clash of light and darkness and which begins by classifying the two actors of the poetic drama in the following terms:

> Je suis la Journée
> Vous, Amy, le Jour

The pairing of *Jour* with *Journée* is particularly interesting. Not only does it make the use of the technique of sub-rhyme by means of a polyptoton, it also introduces into the grammatical structure of the poem a feminine counterpart to the *Jour*. [11] The dependent role of *Journée* is underlined by the morpheme *-née,* which, owing to its formal resemblance to the past participial morpheme, gives a passive quality to the Lover here (a passive which is in sharp contrast to the dynamic role of the poetess who is the creator of the poem). The form *Journée* further underlines the ascendency of *Jour* because of the former's connotation of duration and waiting so that a semantic, as well as a quasi-grammatical relationship, is formed by the pairing of the two words. *Journée* is literally the recipient of *Jour*; she is the one who awaits the coming of the *Jour,* she is the one who receives him and makes him an integral part of her.

> Je suis la Journee,
>> Vous, Amy, le Jour,
>> Qui m'a destournee
>> Du fascheux sejour.
> D'aymer la Nuict certes je ne veulx point,
> Pource qu'à vice elle vient toute appoint:
>> Mais à vous toute estre
>> Certes je veulx bien,
>> Pource qu'en vostre estre
>> Ne gist que tout bien
>>> Là où en tenebres
>> On ne peult rien veoir
>> Que choses funebres,
>> Qui font peur avoir,
> On peult de nuict encor se resjouyr

---

[11] See Robert Griffin, "Pernette Du Guillet's Response to Scève: a Case for Abstract Love," *Esprit créateur,* V, 45, 1965, pp. 110-116. However for a different interpretation, see T. A. Perry, "Pernette Du Guillet's poetry of love and Desire," *BHR,* vol. 35, 1973, pp. 259-271.

De leurs amours faisant amantz jouyr:
    Mais la jouyssance
    De folle pitié
    N'a point de puissance
    Sur nostre amytié,
      Veu qu'elle est fondée
    En prosperité
    Sur Vertu sondée
    De toute equité.
  La nuict ne peult un meurtre declarer,
Comme le jour, qui vient à esclairer
    Ce que la nuict cache,
    Faisant mille maulx,
    Et ne veult qu'on sache
    Ses tours fins, et caultz.
     La nuict la paresse
    Nourrit, qui tant nuit:
    Et le jour nous dresse
    Au travail, qui duit.
  O heureux jour, bien te doit estimer
Celle qu'ainsi as voulu allumer,
    Prenant tousjours cure
    Reduire à clarté
    Ceulx que nuict obscure
    Avoit escarté!
     Ainsi esclairee
    De si heureux jour,
    Seray asseurée
    De plaisant sejour.

As is traditional, light here is the enemy and antithesis of darkness. However the natural antagonism of these two opposites is further enriched with a moral and spiritual dimension. This is one of the few cases in Du Guillet's poetry where her use of chiaroscuro implies the contrast between physical and spiritual love, as in Scève's verse, and where darkness is seen not just as an undesirable state but as a possible temptation to the Lover. However, the negative qualities of night are not limited to the domain of love but extend to all aspects of the moral realm, from the gravest of crimes, murder (which night conceals, day reveals) to the relatively trivial sloth (night encourages laziness while day fosters the useful). Since each attribute of daylight is implicitly linked to the virtue of the Beloved, the pure light his love sheds is an inspiration not only to love but to virtue itself and so the purity of the Beloved is reminiscent of the purity associated with the sun, that all-seeing eye of the universe of which Phèdre's sin made her so fearful.

While the main characteristics of the aggressive eye topos are absent from this type of light imagery (although the eyes are implicitly and often explicitly involved), the topos itself does make a rather curious appearance in *Chanson* VI of the *Rymes*. Robert Griffin has called the passion of which Du Guillet speaks in her poetry a case of "abstract love" and indeed his contention appears to be borne out in this poem where it is not Cupid, the God of sensual love who conquers the Lover, but Virtue. Nonetheless in a highly original manipulation of the topos, Cupid is finally associated with Virtue but with the clear stipulation that Virtue remains supreme. In other words, we are dealing with what is above all a spiritual love here, whereas when the aggressive eye topos appears, it usually has sensual overtones, even when ideal love is the primary goal. In Du Guillet's poetry the sensual element is indeed present as T. A. Perry has shown, but it is more often replaced by spiritual and abstract love than is the case with most other poets of the *Ecole lyonnaise*. [12] So it is in her sixth *Chanson*. In an echo of both Petrarch [13] and Scève, [14] Du Guillet depicts her persona's metaphorical "springtime." What is usually the time of sensual desires and encounters [15] is for her a time devoid of knowledge, real freedom and even deep feeling:

> Sans congnoissance aucune en mon Printemps j'estois:
> Alors aucun souspir encor point ne gectois
> Libre sans liberté: car rien ne regrectois
>   En ma vague pensée
> De molz, et vains desirs follement dispensée.

---

[12] This can be seen clearly if we compare her use of the light/darkness antithesis with Scève's use of the same imagery. For Scève, the conflict between light and darkness is often associated with the struggle between sensual and ideal love, whereas for Du Guillet, usually darkness is either representative of the absence of the Beloved, or of the state of utter nothingness in which the Lover found herself before ideal love enlightened the loveless life.

[13] Petrarch, *Rime,* 325, 13: "Ch'era de l'anno e di mi 'etate aprile [. . .]" quoted in Maurice Scève, *Délie,* ed. I. D. McFarlane (Cambridge 1966), p. 369.

[14] Scève, *Délie* (op. cit.), dizain VI: "Libre vivois en l'Avril de mon aage [. . .]."

[15] Scève, dizain I: "L'œil trop ardent en mes jeunes erreurs / Girouettoit mal cault, à l'impourveue [. . .]."

Into this emotional and intellectual vacuum comes Cupid, who, making use of eyes (and it is not clear from the text whether they are his eyes, the speaker's, or those of somebody else), tries to bring her under his sway:

> Mais Amour, tout jaloux du commun bien des Dieux
> Se voulant rendre à moy, comme à maintz, odieux,
> Me vint escarmoucher par faulx alarmes d'yeulx,
>     Mais je veis sa fallace:
> Parquoy me retiray, et luy quictay la place.

Here the familiar violating glance is for once ineffectual and in spite of repeated attacks, Cupid, usually irresistible, is unable to inflame his intended victim:

> Je vous laisse penser, s'il fut alors fasché:
> Car depuis en maintz lieux il s'est tousjours caché,
> Et, quand à descouvert m'a veure, m'a lasché
>     Maintz traictz à la volée:
> Mais onc ne m'en sentis autrement affolée.

In desperation, Cupid, God of sensual love, turns to the arrows and archers of *Vertu,* here representing above all virtuous love, hoping the wound they inflict will allow him entry into the Lover's soul (the *elle* in the following passage refers to *Vertu*):

> [ . . .]
> Mais elle ne permit qu'on me feist aultre oultrage,
> Fors seulement blesser chastement mon courage,
> Dont Amour escumoit et d'envie, et de rage:
>     O bien heureuse envie,
> Qui pour un si hault bien m'a hors de moy ravie.

The entry of chaste love into the speaker's soul produces some of the same effects sensual love normally brings: she is "hors de (elle) ravie! " and her former state of nothingness has been transformed into a universe of feeling (but chaste feeling) and knowledge. However, she does not undergo the sweet suffering, the love swoon or any of the other physical and emotional symptoms which Cupid's arrows usually bring and while eyes were suggested as the aggressors in Cupid's attack, the arrows of virtuous love appear to go directly to the heart and to bypass the Lover's own eyes. And yet, paradoxically, the Lover is grateful for Cupid's attempted aggression for even if he were unable to have his way with her, it was he who enlisted *Vertu* so that in a sense she has Cupid to thank for her final awakening to the chaste love she now experiences for her Beloved:

> Ne pleures plus, Amour: car à toy suis tenue,
> Veu que par ton moyen Vertu chasse la nue,
> Qui me garda long temps de me congnoistre nue,
>     Et frustrée du bien,
> Lequel, en le goustant, j'ayme, Dieu sçait combien.
>     Ainsi toute aveuglée en tes lyens je vins,
> Et tu me mis es mains, où heureuse devins,
> D'un qui est haultement en ses escriptz divins,
>     Comme de nom, severe,
> Et chaste tellement que chacun l'en revere.

Chaste love, then, in operating its transformation on the Lover's soul, has nonetheless made use of the weapons of Cupid and of sensual love. *Vertu* had its archers who pierced the speaker's heart, *Vertu* captured the speaker who is no less a victim because her captor is chaste love.

In another poem (Epigramme LIV), the temptation of sensual love appears stronger and more menacing than elsewhere in Du Guillet's verse but is conquered by the light of chaste love which illumined the darkness in which the speaker had subsisted before knowing her Beloved. In this poem also we find eye imagery, and here the eye sending out an arrow belongs to *l'inconstant* and is equated with the *erreurs* of sensual love. Here too there is an explicit association of eye imagery with the chiaroscuro antithesis, which is so frequent in Du Guillet's work:

> Celle clarté mouvante sans umbrage,
> Qui m'esclarcit en mes tenebreux jours,
> De sa lueur esblouit l'œil volage
> A l'inconstant pour ne veoir mes sejours:
> Car, me voyant, m'eust consommé tousjours
> Par les erreurs de son errante fleche.

Once again it is the perfect light brought by pure love and the Beloved which is at work here. "Clarté" has been associated with her *Jour* ever since Epigramme II where her eyes had perceived "la clarté à la ronde" (line 9). Not only did this light, presumably beamed from the Beloved's eyes, illumine the Lover's "tenebreux jours," it also dazzled "l'œil volage" which apparently belongs to another suitor seeking to destroy by the arrows of his fiery glance the Speaker's tranquillity. This other eye is indeed aggressive and violating (at least potentially) and the negative connotations of its effect are underlined by the polyptotonic association of *erreurs* and *errante,* which creates a semantic ambiguity as both words are derived from *errare* meaning either "to go astray" or simply to "wander." The juxtaposition of these two semantic fields results in an interchange of meaning: *erreur* can be read as either "errors" or "wanderings," while *errante* is either "wandering," "errant" or "in error." As the notion of "wandering" has already been endowed with a negative value in the expression "l'œil volage," the addition of the connotation "error" completes the negativity equated with the aggressiveness of the eye, which by a perhaps ironic use of intertextuality recalls both the "giovanile errore" of Petrarch and "L'œil trop ardent en mes jeunes erreurs" (itself a reminiscence of Petrarch) of Scève. The reference to Scève's text is amusing because Scève has become the fictional Beloved of the *Rymes,* the incarnation of pure love and light, the antithesis of the concupiscent "œil volage." However the *clarté* of the Beloved's eyes which conquer the rival's fickle glance restores the desire for chaste love and brings new life to the Lover, overcoming the baseness of physical passion associated with the physical eyes.

We can see from this examination of Du Guillet's imagery that while only certain elements of the aggressive eye topos are present in her writing, eye imagery is central to her portrayal of love. Since her favourite metaphor for the Beloved is *Jour* which is associated with light and the sun, it is not a betrayal of the text to see the *clarté* which is a constant of the Beloved's presence as emanating from his eyes and as being consequently associated with the purity of the sun, the eye of the universe. Because of the relationship between the eye and light, the eye is also implicit in her dialectic of light and darkness and in the chiaroscuro imagery she uses to signal the coming of love into her existence. The eyes are still the instigators of love and essential to its sustenance, even if the full panoply of images usually associated with the aggressive eye topos is absent in her poetry.

## Louise Labé

When we turn to Louise Labé's verse, we find a more traditional use of eye imagery. Love, for Labé, is not something almost
totally removed from the physical plane, but a mixture of sensual
and spiritual elements, with a strong emphasis on the physical. The
act of seeing has, after all, two principal implications in Renaissance
love theory. Usually these two are complementary, but they can be
antithetical. Firstly, as we have seen, physical sight can be the symbol of spiritual insight or enlightenment, since the eyes were considered by neo-platonic philosophers to be the principal means by
which knowledge was acquired. This connotation is particularly appropriate to ideal, platonic love whose aim is not physical but spiritual union, and for which even spiritual union is only a means and
not an end, a means of regaining the soul's original understanding
of the Ideas, lost when the soul fell into the material world. Second-
ly, sight often implies physical attraction and is a means of recreating
the corporal image of the Beloved in the mind. In the New Testa-
ment we find reference to the "lust of the eye" (I John 2:16) and
to having "eyes full of adultery" (2 Peter 2:14). It is also significant that in the Sermon on the Mount, the lust of the eye is singled
out as being as reprehensible as adultery:

> Ye have heard that it was said by them of old time, Thou
> shalt not commit adultery: but I say unto you, that
> whosoever looketh on a woman to lust after her hath com-
> mitted adultery with her already in his heart (Matthew
> 5:27-28).

The Church Fathers were equally severe in their warnings against
the "concupiscence des yeux." [16] Even in the neo-platonic concep-
tion of love, it is widely accepted that the initial sight of human
beauty produces physical desire, but that this desire for the material is (or should be) transformed into desire for the spiritual ideal
beauty of which the corporal is but an imperfect reflection. However, any emphasis on the act of seeing in love literature carries
implicitly with it an attraction for the physical in the same way

---

[16] Saint Augustine speaks in the *Confessions* of the eye's concupiscence.
See also Jean Starobinski, *L'œil vivant* (Paris: Gallimard, 1961), p. 14.

that neo-platonic theorising about ideal love was sometimes sub-
verted at the physical level. Just as Simontault can use the neo-
platonic interpretation of the myth of the androgyne as an excuse
for philandering,[17] many of the readers of treatises dealing in whole
or in part with love could conveniently forget that the love in question was any other variety than erotic love. As E. Meylan has remarked in reference to Leone Ebreo's *Dialoghi*:

> Il est vrai que dans leur ensemble, les *Dialogues* ont une
> signification plutôt métaphysique qu'érotique, mais la ma-
> jorité des lecteurs ne les prenait plus dans ce premier
> sens.[18]

So it is that the love described by Labé, despite neoplatonic overtones,[19] is above all a physical and emotional experience rather than
a search for spiritual enlightenment. It is for this reason that the
eyes play a much more concrete role in her poetry than in Du
Guillet's.

In her first elegy, Labé recounts the history of the love experience which is the subject of her poetry. At the outset, the power
of love is set forth in mythological terms: love is *Amour*, Cupid,
and as a sign of his omnipotence he is immediately characterised
as "d'hommes et Dieus vainqueur," the alliterative "d" breaking
down the barriers which usually separate mankind and the gods:

> Au temps qu'Amour, d'hommes et Dieus vainqueur,
> Faisoit bruler de sa flamme mon cœur,
> En embrasant de sa cruelle rage
> Mon sang, mes os, mon esprit et courage

The temporal structure of the poem is based on an alternation between the *past* (expressed by the imperfect) when the flame of
love was burning, and the *present,* when only the bitter-sweet mem-

---

[17] Marguerite de Navarre, *L'Heptaméron,* ed. M. François (Paris: Garnier,
1960), p. 48.

[18] E. Meylan, "L'évolution de la notion d'amour platonique," *Humanisme
et Renaissance,* V, 1938, p. 425.

[19] For an intelligent and useful discussion of Neoplatonic (and Petrarchan)
elements in Labé's vers, see Andrea Chan, "Petrarchism and Neoplatonism in
Louise Labé's Concept of Happiness," *Australian Journal of French Studies,*
XIV, 1977, pp. 213-232.

ory of love remains. This time sequence is juxtaposed with a second past/present antithesis, the past being pre-historic time as far as the act of literary creation is concerned, the present being the exercise of those poetic talents which had been dormant in the past when the love experienced by Labé's persona waxed strong:

> Encore lors je n'avois la puissance
> De lamenter ma peine et ma souffrance
> Encor Phebus, ami des Lauriers vers,
> N'avoit permis que fisse des vers:
> Mais maintenant que sa fureur divine
> Remplit d'ardeur ma hardie poitrine,
> Chanter me fait . . .

However, there is a more distant past in the poem [20] than the past time of her love, for it too had a prehistory. Just as in Du Guillet's poetry the speaker's state before love made itself known to her is described. Whereas the pre-love condition described in Du Guillet's verse was one of darkness and nothingness, Labé's persona enjoyed a period of rugged independence with respect to the chains of love, a period of both superiority over those who succumbed to its power and even of sadistic cruelty by making use of her power to inspire love in others. As this past time is recalled by the speaker, the aggressive eye topos comes into play to describe her power over others. This remembrance of things past reawakens pain and sorrow and it is interesting that the first mention of the eye comes when the painful memory brings tears to her eyes. These tears are the physical antithesis to the fire of love which she first inspired in others and which then overcame her and caused her suffering because the object of her love was as cruel to her as she had been to those who had fallen under the power of her glance:

> Je sens desja un piteus souvenir,
> Qui me contreint la larme à l'œil venir.
> Il m'est avis que je sens les alarmes
> Que premiers j'ù d'Amour, je voy les armes,
> Dont il s'arma en venant m'assaillir:
> C'estoit mes yeus, dont tant faisois saillir

---

[20] See Lawrence Harvey, *The Aesthetics of the Renaissance Love Sonnet* (Geneva: Droz, 1962) for a discussion of the use of time in Labé's work.

De traits, à ceus qui trop me regardoient,
Et de mon arc assez ne se gardoient. [21]

Here we have many of the elements of the aggressive eye tradition: the Lady's eyes are Cupid's weapons and she uses them to
avenge herself of those who look too often and too long at her.
There is visual interaction between the two parties concerned and
the Lady's glance is like arrows (*traits*), aggressive, wounding,
killing. However, in an ironic twist, Cupid in turn takes his own
revenge on her because of her disdain for love. The result is that
these eyes, formerly the aggressors, now become traitors and fall
victim to another glance, allowing Cupid to gain entry to her soul
and domination over it:

Mais ces miens traits, ces miens yeus me defirent,
Et de vengeance estre exemple me firent.
Et, me moquant, et, voyant l'un aymer,
L'autre bruler et d'Amour consommer:
En voyant tant de larmes espandues,
Tant de soupirs et prieres perdues,
Je n'aperçu que soudein me vint prendre
Le mesme mal que je soulois reprendre:
Qui me persa d'une telle furie
Qu'encor n'en suis apres long tems guerie:

Love here is not the uplifting spiritual revelation we found in Du
Guillet's work. It brings only suffering, compensated for, it is true,
by occasional pleasures (as we shall see when we examine Labé's
sonnets) and whose most positive aspect is its stimulus to poetic
creation. Its primarily physical nature is apparent from the pain it
brings (spiritual or ideal love is only momentarily painful) and this
is why the eyes play such a prominent role in the initiation of
Labe's persona to love.

Just as the eyes figure prominently in the first poem of her
elegaic trilogy, so they make an appearance at the very beginning
of her 24 sonnets. Most anthologies omit the first sonnet of the
group since it is in Italian, [22] and J.-J. Salverda de Grave goes so

---

[21] Albert-Marie Schmidt, *Poètes du XVIè siècle* (Paris, 1959). All extracts
from Labé's poems are quoted from this edition unless otherwise stated.
[22] Cf. Schmidt, op. cit., and Floyd Gray, *Anthologie de la poésie française
du XVIè siècle* (New York: Appleton, Century, Croft, 1967). As the Italian

far as to claim that "le fait seul que la pièce est écrite en italien dénonce son caractère factice." [23] However, this sonnet cannot be dismissed so lightly. It is true that the language in which it is written does set it apart from the poems that follow, but it is in fact an epigraph to the whole work and should no more be neglected than the "Vertumnis quotquot sunt natus iniquis" which begins Diderot's *Neveu de Rameau* and which provides an initial insight into the character of its protagonist. An epigraph is rarely a useless ornament but is usually a key or portal to the work which follows. What Labé's Italian sonnet does is to provide a transitional bridge between the elegies and the sonnets. Its opening lines explicitly set the love experience in a mythological framework (the first elegy began with a less explicit mythological reference: "d'hommes et Dieus") with its placing of the persona's love-inspired sorrow in a hyperbolic relationship with that of Ulysses:

> Non hauria Ulysse o qualun qu'altro mai
> Piu accorto fù, da quel divino aspetto
> Pien di gratie, d'honor et di rispetto
> Sperato qual i sento affanni e guai.

And her suffering comes from a wound inflicted by Cupid by means of the beautiful eyes of the Beloved:

> Pur, Amor, co i begli occhi tu fatt' hai
> Tal piaga dentro al mio innocente petto,
> Di cibo et di calor gia tuo ricetto,
> Che rimedio non v'e si tu nel' dai.

Not only do we find an elliptic reworking of the agressive eye topos here (which also echoes its use in the first elegy), but the imagery associated with it leads to an implicit connection between the gaze and the instilling of venom into the Lover's soul (one of the images frequently associated with the power of the eyes):

---

sonnet is in fact the first in the cycle, we have changed the numbering of the sonnets as given by Schmidt so that the first French sonnet of the cycle is numbered 2 by us instead of 1, and so on.

[23] J.-J. Salverda de Grave (ed.), *Œuvres complètes de Louise Labé* (Maestricht, 1928), p. xiii.

O sorte dura, che mi fa esser quale
Punta d'un scorpio, et domandar riparo
Contr'el velen' dall'istesso animale.

In the final tercet, the speaker gives voice to the ambivalent nature
of the passionate love she describes. She asks for relief from her
pain, provided that her desire is not extinguished at the same time,
for paradoxically, while the onslaught of love is likened to a kind
of death, loss of desire is also equated with death, but of a far
more terrible species:

Chieggio li fol (sol?) ancida questa noia,
Non estingua el desir a une si caro,
Che mancar non potra ch'i non mi muoia.

The aggressive role played by the "begli occhi" in inspiring love
is echoed in the French sonnet which follows. This poem represents
the various acts and actions of the comedy of love in a series of
apostrophes referring now to one now to the other partner. Some
are in fact deliberately ambiguous,[24] thus adding to the complexity
of the sweet and painful game which unfolds before us, every move
being introduced by the exclamation "ô," which serves as a kind
of emotional punctuation throughout the sonnet:

O beaux yeus bruns, ô regars destournez,
O chaus soupirs, ô larmes espandues,
O noires nuits vainement atendues,
O jours luisans vainement retournez:
  O tristes pleins, ô desirs obstinez,
O tems perdus, ô peines despendues,
O mile morts en mile rets tendues,
O pires maux contre moy destinez:
  O ris, ô front, cheveux, bras, mains et doits:
O lut pleintif, viole, archet et vois:
Tan de flambeaus pour ardre une femmelle!
  De toy me plein, que, tant de feus portant,
En tant d'endrois, d'iceus mon cœur tatant,
N'en est sur toy volé quelque estincelle.

---

[24] See Nicolas Ruwet, "Analyse structurale d'un poème français," *Linguistics*, 3, January 1964 for an interesting if not always convincing analysis of this sonnet.

The ambiguity of just who is the subject and who the object of the actions implied by the series of nouns makes itself felt in the first two apostrophes of the opening line. Presumably the "beaux yeux bruns" belong to the male partner and the "regard destournez" to the female, and yet this is not necessarily so, particularly as in Labé's poetry we often have a reversal of the roles which are usually attributed to male and female in petrarchan type love poetry.[25] What is important for our purposes here is that the first act of the comedy involves eye play, with each of the parties affecting the other with his or her glance and the other being affected by the same medium. It is also interesting that the exchange of glances (or the attempted exchange) results in the eyes' producing tears of sorrow, so that in the second line of the sonnet, mention is first made of the fire of passion, to be immediately countered by its inimical contrary, water. In Lyonese poetry, there often seems to be an equation which runs as follows: love forces itself upon the soul through the eyes and inflames it; the pain inflicted by love's wound and by the cruelty of the Beloved expresses itself by being expelled through the eyes as tears. Thus love and fire are in a constant relationship to sorrow and tears through the medium of the eyes: "O chaus soupirs, ô larmes espandues."

So great is the suffering engendered by the initial glance of love that in the third sonnet, the tears are hyperbolically swelled into rivers, which spring from the eyes and are the direct result of love's sorrow:

> O longs desirs! O esperances vaines,
> Tristes soupirs et larmes coutumieres
> A engendré de moy maintes rivieres,
> Dont mes deus yeux sont sources et fontaines.

In the rest of the sonnet, love is pictured as using his traditional bow and arrows but without the intermediary of the eyes. Now the Lady is so smitten with love that she can defy Cupid to do his

---

[25] The *Belle cruelle* of the Petrarchan-troubadour tradition is replaced here by the *Beau cruel*; it is the male who is active in inspiring love, but passive and apparently indifferent in receiving it. The female is passive in her reception of love, active in trying to sustain it and yet as she is basically powerless to alter the Beloved's coldness, she finally becomes dependent on his every whim.

worst. She has received so many wounds that there is no more
room on her body for more:

> Qu'encor Amour sur moy son arc essaie,
> Que nouveaus feus me gette et nouveaus dars,
> Qu'il se despite, et pis qu'il pourra face:
>     Car je suis tant navree en toutes pars,
> Que plus en moy une nouvelle plaie
> Pour m'empirer ne pourroit trouver place.

In Sonnets V and VI, the eye plays another role, not directly
associated with the aggressive eye topos and yet depending on a
mutual relationship of glances to further the love experience. In a
variation on the traditional petrarchan theme that the lover, who
endures suffering during the daylight hours and hopes for the relief
sleep usually affords when night comes, in fact discovers that sleep
evades him so that night increases his pain instead of reducing it.
In the quatrains however, Labé's persona addresses a prayer to the
Goddess of Love, symbolised by the planet Venus upon which the
speaker's gaze is turned while she thinks sorrowfully of her love
during the night hours which are usually devoted to sleep. The
planet is asked to gaze in turn upon the sorrowing speaker as she
laments her grief, while the latter keeps her eye fixed on the noc-
turnal symbol of love in the sky. Thus we have a curious interaction
between the gaze of the speaker directed at the personified planet,
while Venus' eyes become the witnesses of her *travaus*. Once again
we find ourselves at the latter end of the love/eyes/heart/eyes/tears
equation, as the eyes send forth their grief in tears. Moreover, it is
the sight of Venus, surrogate for the absent and cruel Beloved,
which acts as an inspiration for the continuation and intensification
of her suffering:

> Clere Venus, qui erres par les Cieus,
> Entans ma vois qui en pleins chantera,
> Tant que ta face au haut du Ciel luira,
> Son long travail et souci ennvieus.
>     Mon œil veillant s'atendrira bien mieus,
> Et plus de pleurs te voyant getera.
> Mieus mon lit mol de larmes baignera,
> De ses travaus voyant témoins tes yeus.
>     Donq des humains sont les lassez esprits
> De dous repos et de sommeil espris.
> J'endure mal tant que le Soleil luit:

> Et quand je suis quasi toute cassee,
> Et que me suis mise en mon lit lassee,
> Crier me faut mon mal toute la nuit.

In the following sonnet, "Clere Venus" is identified directly with the absent Beloved, and eye imagery is used to describe the effect he has on those around him when he is present. His semi-divine nature is stressed by the name he is given: "ce cler Astre," and while the epithet *cler* and the nouns *Astre* associate him with the "Clere Venus" of the preceding poem, Labé has chosen a masculine word for star to underline the fact that the metaphor is a metonymy for the Beloved. Honour and joy are the gifts bestowed by this godlike creature when he casts his benificent glances upon some lucky woman:

> Deus ou trois fois bienheureus le retour
> De ce cler Astre, et plus heureus encore
> Ce que son œil de regarder honore:
> Que celle là recevroit un bon jour,
>     Qu'elle pourroit se vanter d'un bon tour
> Qui baiseroit le plus beau don de Flore,
> Le mieus sentant que jamais vid Aurore,
> Et y feroit sur ses levres sejour!

The idealised picture of the Beloved presented here with a perhaps a touch of bitter irony is transformed in the tercets by the introduction of a new element: the speaker's jealousy. Here we witness the aggressive use of the eyes by the Lover in an attempt to gain conquest over the Beloved and to take revenge on him for transmitting his love so generously to any *celle là* who chances to look at him:

> C'est à moy seule à qui ce bien est du,
> Pour tant de pleurs et tant de tems perdu:
> Mais, le voyant, tant luy feray de feste,
>     Tant emploiray de mes yeus le pouvoir,
> Pour dessus lui plus de credit avoir
> Qu'en peu de tems feray grande conqueste.

The serene, curiously passive and complacent glance of the Beloved suddenly stands in sharp contrast to the Lover's eyeplay, which is dynamic, aggressive and self-serving. After having succumbed to the power of his *begli occhi,* she tries to avenge herself by making use of the same weapons against him, just as Leander did (successfully) when he was first wounded by Hero's gaze. [26] As in all of Labé's sonnets, the success of such counter-attacks is presented in an understated, hypothetical way by the use of the future tense. Her love is a dialectic between the sorrow of unrequited love and the hope of future reciprocal love. In this sonnet, as elsewhere, the present refers only to general statements, not to states of present reality, and so even the happiness of the *celle là* of the quatrains is placed in the hypothetical conditional, suggesting that the state of affairs described by the present is ideal rather than actual.

This is quite explicit in Sonnet X, which although it does not use eye imagery, depends on the act of seeing. Sight becomes a metaphor for desire and the Lover's wish for possession and reciprocity is eloquently expressed in the parallel grammatical structure to be found in the quatrains. This structure runs counter to the form of the sonnet, where the octet usually forms a grammatical and semantic unit. Here, we find two parallel clauses of approximately equal length being assigned the first seven lines of the sonnet, instead of occupying the complete octet. This compression of the two temporal clauses beginning with "quand" divides the sonnet into two equal parts (7 + 7), rather than the usual division (8 + 6) and bears numerical testimony to the perfection of the Beloved. [27] This unusual and effective manipulation of traditional formal structures is made possible by the anaphoric opening of each section: "Quand j'aperçoy ton blond chef [...]" and "quand je te vois orné [...]." The parallelism is enhanced not only by the grammatical similarity (each clause has a conjunction plus personal pronoun plus verb) but also because of the rhyme between *aperçoy* and *vois* and the fact that, by the addition of the pronoun object at the beginning of the second clause, both initial sequences have four syllables:

> Quand j'aperçoy ton blond chef, couronné
> D'un laurier verd, faire un Lut si bien pleindre,
> Que tu pourrois à te suivre contreindre
> Arbres et rocs: quand je te vois, orné

---

[26] See the extract from Musaeus, *Hero and Leander* quoted in chapter 1 of this study, p. 18.

[27] See Harvey, op. cit., pp. 52-3.

> Et de vertus dix mile environné,
> Au chef d'honneur plus haut que nul ateindre,
> Et des plus hauts les louenges esteindre,
> Lors dit mon cœur en soy passionné:
>     Tant de vertus qui te font estre aymé,
> Qui de chacun te font estre estimé,
> Ne te pourroient aussi bien faire aymer?
>     Et, ajoutant à ta vertu louable
> Ce nom encor de m'estre pitoyable,
> De mon amour doucement t'enflamer?

The association *voir-désirer* leads back to a variant of the aggressive eyes topos in Sonnet XI, where the Beloved's eyes are once again the aggressors, while the Lover's eyes have become passive receptors of the arrows cast forth by the Other's gaze. The topos here is part of another theme, the conflict between heart and eyes, which is usually based on the fact that since love makes the heart suffer, the eyes are therefore traitors for having allowed admittance to love. Here precisely the opposite occurs, since it is the heart which betrays the eyes by spoiling with the pangs of love the pleasure they experience when contemplating the Beloved's beauty. In this case the usual eye imagery is combined with a garden metaphor, in a reminiscence of the garden in the *Roman de la Rose*. In this poem the arrow imagery is in a sense one step removed from the eyes, since they are first metamorphosed to become "petits jardins pleins de fleurs amoureuses." As the eyes of the Beloved have been qualified in the first line by the epithet "pleins de beauté," there is a direct correlation between the physical attractiveness of the Beloved and the "fleurs amoureuses." Here, as elsewhere in Labé's poetry the importance of the eye in love is shown by the fact that it becomes a synecdoche for both the Beloved and the Lover herself. The actors in this drama of love are reduced to what Jean Starobinski (after Jean-Jacques Rousseau) would call "yeux vivants," the one exercising its power of fascination over the other by instilling the image of love and desire through the gateway of the soul. It is precisely in these beloved eyes that danger lurks, for the *locus amoenus* they represent also conceals Cupid's arrows, ready to wound and possess the Lover without granting the favour of mutual possession. It is significant that while the eyes of the Beloved are conceived as a plurality: "O dous regards, ô yeus pleins de beauté," The Lover is but a single eye, so steadfastly is her gaze fixed on the object of fascination. Here too, the eyes produce tears as a result of their having contemplated the Beloved but the blame is attributed to the heart since it is from the heart that the sorrow of love proceeds:

> O dous regard, o yeus pleins de beauté,
> Petits jardins pleins de fleurs amoureuses
> Où sont d'Amour les flesches dangereuses,
> Tant à vous voir mon œil s'est arresté!
>     O cœur felon, o rude cruauté,
> Tant tu me tiens de façons rigoureuses,
> Tant j'ay coulé de larmes langoureuses
> Sentant l'ardeur de mon cœur tourmenté!
>     Doncques, mes yeus, tant de plaisir avez,
> Tant de bons tours par ses yeus recevez:
> Mais toy, mon cœur, plus les vois s'y complaire,
>     Plus tu languiz, plus en as de souci:
> Or devinez si je suis aise aussi,
> Sentant mon œil estre à mon cœur contraire.

Arrow imagery reappears several sonnets later in Sonnet XIX, and although it is used independently of its usual association with the eyes, if we read the poem in the macrocontext of the sonnet cycle, the arrow metaphor implies the eyes' role in love. Here the arrows are not Cupid's but are assimilated into the framework of a hunting scene in which Diana at first plays the leading part. When Diana and her nymphs unexpectedly come across the dejected speaker of the poem, they are astonished at seeing her without arrows and quiver, and one of them asks her why she has no weapons:

> Je m'animay, repons je, à un passant,
> Et lui getay en vain toutes mes flesches
> Et l'arc apres: mais lui, les remassant,
> Et les tirant me fit cent et cent bresches.

Once again the speaker's arrows have proven ineffectual against their prey and have been used by the Beloved to wound her. It is obvious that this is a thinly veiled metaphor (one could almost call it an allegory) for the failure of the speaker's gaze to capture the Other and the subsequent treachery of the eyes in allowing the soul to be wounded by love. We have a variant of the predicament set forth in the first Elegy: "Mais ces miens traits, ces miens yeus me defirent."

The final appearance of eye imagery in Labé's sonnets comes in the second-to-last poem of her sequence, Sonnet XXIII. Here the metaphor is not used by the poet to describe the suddenness and irresistible nature of love. It is presented as an image used by the Beloved to praise the Lady. In view of his absence from her now, it becomes a sign of his duplicity. In the Beloved's discourse as reported by the speaker, he compared (and the past definite is used to express this completed action, thus placing it in a completed past framework) her eyes to suns from which Cupid shot arrows to wound him with love. Once again the poem has a temporal frame-work which juxtaposes these grandiose and beguiling statements of the past with the sad reality of the present. The tears which the Beloved claimed were caused by the intensity of his love, tears used presumably as a weapon to assure his conquest of his Lover, have long since dried up. The Beloved's lack of constancy is underlined by the contrast between the high rhetoric he used to declare his love and his present indifference and absence. His frivolous use of a metaphor with as many philosophical and physical ramifications as that of the aggressive eye is the ultimate sign of his falsehood:

> Las! que me sert que si parfaitement
> Louas jadis et ma tresse doree,
> Et de mes yeus la beauté comparee
> A deus Soleils, dont l'Amour finement
>     Tira les trets, causez de ton tourment?
> Où estes-vous, pleurs de peu de duree?
> Et Mort par qui devoit estre honoree
> Ta ferme amour et iteré serment?

The poem concludes with a statement that expresses both sorrow for the speaker's bitterness and a vengeful hope that the Beloved is suffering the sorrows of love at the hands of another woman, just as she, the speaker, is suffering because of him:

> Donques c'estoit le but de ta malice
> De m'asservir sous ombre de service?
> Pardonne moy, Ami, à cette fois,
>     Estant outree et de despit et d'ire:
> Mais je m'assure, quelque part que tu sois,
> Qu'autant que moy tu soufres de martire.

The "je m'asseure" of line 13 indicates hope rather than certainty

and should be understood quite literally as "I assure myself" and
not "I am sure," otherwise Labé could just as easily have written
"je suis sure" with no detriment to the metre.

There is one more place in Labé's work where eye imagery
appears and this example at first seems to undermine the importance
attributed in her poetry to the eyes' role in love. In the only prose
work she is known to have written, the interesting and unusual
*Débat de Folie et d'Amour,* we discover what appears to be a
disparaging reference to the topos:

> Et pour commencer à la belle premiere naissance
> d'Amour, qu'y ha il plus despourvu de sens, que la per-
> sonne à la moindre ocasion du monde vienne en Amour,
> en recevant une pomme comme Cydipee? en lisant un
> livre, comme la Dame Francisque de Rimini? en voyant,
> en passant, se rende si tot serve et esclave, et conçoive
> esperance de quelque grand bien sans savoir s'il en y ha?
> Dire que c'est la force de l'œil de la chose aymee, et que
> de là sort une sutile evaporacion ou sang, que nos yeus
> reçoivent, et entre jusques au cœur: ou, comme pour loger
> un nouvel hoste, faut pour luy trouver sa place, mettre tout
> en desordre. Je say que chacun le dit: mais s'il est vray
> j'en doute. Car plusieurs ont aymé sans avoir à cette oca-
> sion, comme le jeune Gnidien, qui ayma l'euvre fait par
> Praxitelle. Quelle influxion pouvoit il recevoir d'un œil
> marbrin? Quelle sympathie y avoit il de son naturel chaud
> et ardent par trop, avec une froide et morte pierre? Qu'est
> ce donq qui l'enflammoit? Folie, qui estoit logee en son
> esprit. Tel feu estoit celui de Narcisse. Son œil ne recevoit
> pas le pur sang et sutil de son cœur mesme; mais la fole
> imaginacion du beau pourtrait, qu'il voyoit en la fonteine,
> le tourmentoit. Exprimez tant que voudrez la force d'un
> œil: faites le tirer mile traits par jour: n'oubliez qu'une
> ligne qui passe par le milieu, jointe avec le sourcil est un
> vray arc: que ce petit humide, que lon voit luire au milieu
> est le trait prest à partir: si est ce que toutes ces flesches
> n'iront en autres cœurs, que ceus que Folie aura pre-
> parez.[28]

However, the speaker here is Mercury, known for his ruse and
cunning. It is his task to defend Folie from the charge that she has
curbed Cupid's power by putting out his eyes and covering them

---

[28] Louise Labé, *Euvres* (Lyon, 1824), p. 59.

with a blindfold which cannot be removed. As Mercury stated earlier in his brief for the defense: "Mon intencion sera de montrer qu'en tout celà Folie n'est rien inferieure à Amour, et qu'Amour ne seroit rien sans elle." [29] In order to show how Folie is the natural and inevitable partner of Cupid, Mercury must, according to the traditions of judicial eloquence, minimise the importance and power of Love's traditional attributes. By seeming to ridicule the aggressive eye topos, Mercury is in fact giving further attestation to its power and omnipresence in the literature of love. In fact, Mercury is not really denying the traditional effect of the love glance. He is merely pointing out that there is an additional factor which is operative in the *innamoramento,* a factor which can even work independently of the eyes on those rare occasions when an inanimate object becomes the Beloved. Mercury's argument is that, unless Folie has already prepared the heart of the Beholder, the glance will be ineffectual, hence Folie and Amour are inseparable. So Labé, even assuming that Mercury is her *porte-parole* (which is not at all certain since Mercury is speaking for Folie, who like Erasmus's personification is a creature whose opinions and actions are sometimes more reasonable than those dictated by human reason, sometimes less), is not reneging on what she has said in her poetry of the eyes' power in love. She is merely adding another dimension to it and in the tradition of a Renaissance philosophical dialogue, attempting to present all sides of the question. Cupid may be a somewhat pathetic figure in the *Débat* since he must be accompanied by Folie, who is ordered to serve as his guide. However, his frightening power over men, women and the gods is in no way diminished, only made more capricious than before because he can no longer see his victims. And in any case, in Labé's poetry (and she is above all a poetess), love is still, with no qualifications whatsoever, "d'hommes et Dieus vainqueur."

## Olivier de Magny

Olivier de Magny is sometimes proposed as the mysterious Beloved who appears in Labé's poetry and those who like to indulge in this type of literary detective work have been quick to point out

---

[29] Ibid., p. 50.

that the Beloved of Labé's work is closely associated with the art of writing poetry.[30] Even if this were so, the coupling of Labé and Magny to form a poetic duo makes even less sense than in the case of Du Guillet and Scève, where it does have some biographical and textual (minimal in our opinion) justification, although it sheds little or no light on their respective poetry. For our purposes, the only link between Labé and Magny is of a thematic nature, for Magny accords an important place in his work to the relationship between the eyes and falling in love. While he does not use eye imagery with the same relative frequently as Labé (although there are, numerically, more examples of such metaphors in his sonnets than in Labé's, since his sonnet cycle numbers 102 poems while hers only contains 24 sonnets and 3 elegies), it is significant that at the supremely important moments of his poetic itinerary, eye imagery comes to the fore. His sonnet sequence opens with a poem, which, while its structure is based on the petrarchan antithesis of cold/heat and fire/ice, is also an invitation to the reader to see the Lady who is the subject of the cycle and to recognise her beauty and the devastating effect it exercises on the poet's persona:

> Regarde après mon corps jà consumé,
> Il le verra vivement alumé
> Du cler rayon de sa beauté celeste.
>   Et cognoistra que sa dure froideur
> Alume en moy la devorante ardeur
> Et le brazier qui me brusle et moleste.[31]

Right at the outset, the eye of the reader is given an important participatory role in Magny's poetry, but it is in the second sonnet of the series that the mysterious workings of the Beloved's eyes are expounded. Developing the notion of the "cler rayon de sa beauté céleste" and of the ardour concealed beneath the ice of the Lady's

---

[30] For example in Labé's sonnet "Quand j'aperçoy ton blond chef," there is an implicit identification of the Beloved with Apollo and with Orpheus. Likewise, in Sonnet XXII, that the Beloved had formerly compared the Lady's eyes to "deus Soleils, dont l'Amour finement / Tira les trets, causez de ton tourment?," would seem to indicate the voice of a poet rather that that of an ordinary mortal. For the identification of Magny with Labé's Beloved, see Guillot, op. cit., p. 67.

[31] Olivier de Magny, *Les Cent Deux Sonnets des Amours,* ed. M. Whitney (Geneva: Droz, 1970), p. 25.

cruelty, the poet concentrates his imagery upon her eyes which are associated with fire, light and lightning, so that they become both the instruments by which love is transmitted and at the same time the cause of love's sufferings. In an interesting variation of the usual arrow imagery which expresses this phenomenon, the eyebrows are pictured as fiery bolts of lightning which penetrate the Lover's heart, and instead of Cupid's being an external agent of love and in some sense its initiator, it is the Lady who is supreme. Her flashing thunderbolts wake the slumbering Cupid, who, like Labé's Folie, is already in the Lover's heart, waiting only to be aroused:

> Les raiz flambans de vostre œil foudroyant,
> Persans mon cueur de leur lumiere prompte,
> Firent lever l'Amour qui me surmonte,
> Qui sommeilloit en mon sein larmoyant.

The adjectival present participle stresses both the power and the suddenness of the rays projected from the Lady's eyes but also, through the association with Jupiter's thunderbolts, attests to her god-like qualities. Here, as in Labé's verse, there is an association between fire and water, since the Lady's eyes dart forth fire which awakens Cupid slumbering in the tear-filled breast of the Lover.

When Cupid does awaken, he quickly takes the initiative and subjugates the Speaker:

> Luy esveillé, freschement flamboyant,
> Tira vers soy la lueur qui me domte,
> Puis en forma une image à ma honte,
> Tous mes espritz à son aise ployant.

His activity is associated with that of the Lady's eyes by the use of alliteration: the "freschement flamboyant" of line 5 recalls "flambans ... foudroyant" of line 1, not only by the coincidence of the initial consonants but also by the fact that within each group there is a *rime pauvre* ([ã]) and each pair of words rhymes in the same way with the other pair. In addition to the phonetic relationship, there is also a semantic similarity between three of the words: *flamboyant, flambans* and *foudroyant*. Once in control of the Lover's heart, Cupid fashions the rays which have penetrated the Lover's soul into a permanent *image* of the Beloved and with this visual repro-

duction firmly implanted on the Lover's heart, his complete subjection is assured.

However, unlike the love-state described in Labé's poems,
Magny's presentation stresses an equal measure of sorrow and joy
and is not strongly tilted towards the sufferings of love as is hers.
This antithetical and paradoxical state is expressed in the sestet in
terms of light, so that once again the speaker's eyes (by implication)
and the Beloved's eyes play the primary role in this scene of rejuvenating *fascinatio:*

> Et neanmoins si douce fut à l'heure
> Ceste clarté des clartez la meilleure,
> Si douce aussi l'idole, et ces beaux yeux,
>     Que tout l'amer qui depuis m'ensorcelle
> Est temperé de ce doux gracieux,
> Qui dans mon cueur tousjours se renouvelle.

The *amer* of line 13 which bewitched him through the medium of
her gaze is tempered by the *doux gracieux* which also emanates
from her eyes. Love is not only suffering but is also a means of
renewal and elevation here, so that we return to one of the principle tenets of the neoplatonic-petrarchan philosophy of love.

The *innamoramento* is also the subject of the less successful
Sonnet 5. Here, although the eyes are not specifically mentioned,
their role is implied, as the experience is once more presented as a
function of light and bedazzlement. The description of the event is
more traditional since it is here Cupid who is totally responsible for
the speaker's falling in love:

> Le jour tant beau et tant aventureux
> Qu'Amour domta ma forte liberté,
> Bruslant mon cueur d'une ardante clarté,
> Qui m'esblouyt, et me rend bien heureux.

The Beloved is presented metonymically as a sun and is associated
with the image of a garden in much the same way as in Labé's
sonnet XI. Here, unfortunately, this image is not tightly incorporated into the metaphorical structure as was the case in her poem
and so becomes little more than a hyperbolic comparison:

> Un beau Soleil, un Soleil vigoureux
> Je vy çà bas, qui d'une infinité

De belles fleurs, en toute extremité,
Ornoit l'entour de ses pas amoureux.

The rather pedestrian octet is followed by an even less successful
sestet, where the poet totally abandons the "Soleil/clarté" imagery
of the quatrains (without ever having developed them in any poetically meaningful way) and turns instead to a petrarchan cliché
which has the Lover following the "pas amoureux" of the Beloved,
only to be ensnared by her hair:

Dont moy oyant le son de ses propos,
M'habandonnay tout soudain le repos,
Et pas à pas mesurois son aleure:
    Mais en suivant si divine excellance,
Trop obstiné dessus sa contenance,
Lyé je fuz avec sa chevelure.

Whitney sees this poem as a "quasi-traduction de la *Canzone 3* de
Sannazar" [32] but while there are some points in common between
the imagery of the two poets, the movement of their respective
works is quite different and the dissimilarities are much more strik-
ing than the resemblances. Perhaps Magny's poem would have been
more satisfactory had he in fact "imitated" Sannazar more faithfully,
as the balance of poetic quality is clearly in favour of the latter.

    In the eleventh sonnet of his cycle, Magny returns to eye imagery
by associating it with the metaphor of the Phoenix. The Beloved
is apostrophised as "mon Phenix," and although according to
Whitney, [33] the word is used to mean "personne unique en son
genre," the traditional attributes of the mythical bird link it with
the fire imagery already present in the first sonnet of the series.
Here the Phoenix sends forth "traits d'œil" which bring either joy
or sadness to the Beholder without altering the intensity of his
love's flame. The implicit association of the Beloved with fire in
this Phoenix metaphor now finds its echo in the Lover's own state.
It is in fact a condition of "immortel feu" in which he finds himself, the "immortel" suggesting both his constancy in love and the
Phoenix's property of being able to be regenerated through fire:

---

[32] Ibid., p. 30.
[33] Ibid., p. 37.

Qu'esperez-vous, mon Phenix, pour me faire
Ore un joyeux, ore un triste trait d'œil,
Si par cela, ma douleur et mon deuil,
Et mon grand feu ne s'estaint ou modere?
   L'immortel feu qui dedans moy repaire
Sort de mon cueur, et vostre doux acueil,
Ou la froideur d'aucun mauvais recueil
N'ont le povoir de l'esteindre et deffaire.

The poem ends rather lamely with a vow of perpetual love but recapitulates the image of Cupid the Archer already used in Sonnet IV, [34] here associating it directly with the first sight of the Beloved:

Regardez donc si jamais homme ayma
Ainsi que moy, que l'archer transforma
Dès le moment que j'euz veu vostre face.
   D'autant qu'en loz, en honneur, et beauté
Vous excellez, en ferme loyauté
Mon amytié toutes autres surpasse.

The following sonnet recapitulates and elaborates on the image of the Archer, this time likening him directly to the Beloved's eyes. The poet then applies to the Lover himself the image of the Phoenix as both a sign of the immortality of his love and also of the beneficient effect love has upon him, since he now partakes of the very nature of his Lady and is constantly revivified. The light from the Lady's eyes is both fiery and divine:

Divine ardeur, flamme amoureuse et belle,
Qui des beaux yeux de ma Dame en mon cueur
Avec ses mains l'Archerot nu vainqueur
Alume prompt d'une sorte nouvelle,

---

[34] Sonnet IV, which is a fairly unexceptional *éloge* of the Beloved's beauty, does give some prominence to the description of the Lady's eyes: "Beau front, beaux yeux de deux arcz couronnez" and talks of "mile rais qui sortent de voz yeux." However, the aggressiveness usually associated with the glance is here applied to the Lady's breast, which gives a rather comical erotic twist to the poem (comical to the modern reader at least), probably not intended by Magny, as he describes the "sein sans per" as the weapon used by the Archer to pierce him: "Je trouve en vous toutes beautez, ma Dame, / Beau front, beaux yeux de deux arcz couronnez, / Soubs deux rubis de lis environnez, / Ces belles dens qui tenaillent mon ame, / Le sein sans per, dont l'Archerot m'entame...."

> Combien Amour et sa mere immortelle
> Je doy louer, ayant de ceste ardeur
> Favorisé de mon sort la froideur,
> Au seul plaisir d'une maistresse telle

In spite of the Lady's paradoxical coldness, [35] his love continues eternal, whether it be faced with the fire of reciprocity or the ice of indifference, the two traditional antitheses being forged into an unusual unity by the power of love:

> Jamais ne soit que cest aspre chaleur
> N'ayt dedans moy lieu, repos, et valeur,
> Jamais ne soit que je n'arde et englace,
>    Puisqu'en bruslant je suis fait immortel,
> Et en glassant je suis encore tel,
> Pour avoir mis mon ame en haulte place.

The miraculous effect exercised on the Lover by the Beloved's glance does not reappear until Sonnet XXXIII. This poem is constructed on the basic comparison between the Lady's eyes and the sun, but here it is enriched by an additional simile in which the Lover is likened to the sunflower which only shows signs of movement and life when the sun is present. This double comparison is embellished by a pun on the alternate French word for the sunflower (usually *tournesol* or *soleil*), *souci,* which evokes the Lover's troubled state when the Beloved is absent. The Lady's glance, like the sun, brings new life to the languishing Lover and her eyes are represented as "ce mien fatal, et celeste flambeau," expressing their likeness to the sun and insisting on their divine origin, while at the same time stressing the inevitability of the poet's present state:

> Comme la fleur qu'on nomme le soucy
> Ternid, et pend sa teste languissante,
> Quand ell' n'est plus du soleil jouyssante,
> Et que le Ciel a son voile obscurcy,
>    Qui toutesfois au matin éclercy
> Par le vermeil de l'aube estincelante,
> Renaist et prend sa couleur excellante,
> Tant que Phebus nous aparoist icy,

---

[35] One cannot help wonder how a phoenix can be cold!

Tout ainsi, las! l'ame et cueur on m'arrache,
Quand le soleil de ma vie on me cache,
J'entens vostre œil si divinement beau.
   Puis je sens bien que je suis renaissant
Incontinent que m'est aparoissant
Ce mien fatal, et celeste flambeau.

When the poet dwells on the beauty of his Beloved and the devastating effect it has on him, the prominent role played by the eyes recurs as a leitmotif. So in Sonnet XLI, in a portrait of the Lady which is at the same time a graphic portrayal of the tyranny of love exercised through beauty, we find a reappearance of the principal functions attributed to the eyes in love:

Ces yeux après, les fleches, retz, et flammes,
Dequoy Amour blesse, prend, et enflamme
Les cueurs, helas, des dolens bien-heureux.
   Mais si pitié parmy ces saintes graces
Il rencontroit, ò sort avantureux!
Un plus grand heur je croy que tu n'embrasses.

They are arrows, trappers ensnaring their victim with nets and flames, igniting the Lover's heart with passion. They are also the God of Love's privileged tools and in the first tercet of the sonnet, devoted completely to the eyes, Magny establishes the eyes' powers as a kind of trinity by a limited use of the technique of *vers rapportés*. Thus *fleches* is dependent on the verb *blesse* (*Amour* being its subject) in the following verse, likewise *retz* is coupled with *prend* and *flammes* with *enflamme*. As the last line of the first tercet suggests, love and the suffering it brings are ambivalent, at once negative and positive and so it is with love's messengers and agents, the eyes. If they usually stun, dazzle, capture, inflame and wound, they also bring illumination, knowledge and even healing.

This side of the eyes' magic powers is presented in Sonnet LXI where Magny's Lover is described as nigh unto death and his spirit ready to leave his "charnelle masse" to fly to the heavens. The eyes, although once again pictured as snares and as arrows, instil, through love, renewed vigour into the Lover's enfeebled spirit and snatch him from death's grasp. At first, they appear to be part of a neoplatonic concept of love. However, in a curious mixture of the spiritual and the erotic, Magny reveals his hand in the final tercet

of the sonnet by using the power he has attributed to the eyes as
a means of persuading the Lady to grant the Lover not merely a
glance but a kiss. Nevertheless it is the eyes which have the lion's
share of the poem's action:

> Peu s'en faloit que mes foibles espritz
> N'eussent laissé ceste charnelle masse,
> Et dedaignans residance si basse,
> Dressé leur vol au celeste pourpris,
>     Lorsque ces yeux (la rethz dont je fus pris)
> D'un seul regard coulorerent ma face,
> Si qu'à l'instant ma foiblesse s'efface,
> Et de vigueur je me senty surpris.
>     Si donc un trait des beaux yeux de ma Reine,
> M'oste des bras de la mort qui m'entreine,
> Et me remet en force entierement,
>     Ne me feroit un baiser de sa bouche
> Domter la mort qui tous animaux touche,
> Et de tant d'heur vivre eternellement?

The beneficient effect of the Lady's glance is also in evidence
in one of the closing sonnets of the *Amours*. Here the brightness
of her gaze eclipses even the sun and a quasi-religious anaphor
popular in love poetry: "Heureux [...]" (a variant of the *beatus
qui* or *felix qui*) transforms the sonnet into a litany of praise which
sums up the powerful benefits of the love experience. Here, once
again the Lady's glance is seen as both a source of light and a
wounding arrow, and the whole octet is devoted to its description
and to its effects, so that it is once more a synecdoche for the whole
person of the Beloved:

> Si ferme foy repose en ceste veuë,
> Dont la clarté fait cacher le soleil,
> Heureux cent fois le regard nompareil,
> Qui de langueur a mon ame pourveuë.
>     Heureux le trait lequel à l'impourveuë
> Persa mon cueur, heureux ce teinct vermeil,
> Qui me servit de premier apareil,
> Au grief ennuy de la playe receuë. [36]

The vicissitudes of love are also expressed through eye imagery
several sonnets later in Sonnet XCIII. Here the entire first quatrain

---

[36] Magny, op. cit., Sonnet XCI, ll. 1-8, p. 112.

is devoted to describing the eyes' power, before their effects are
dealt with later in the poem. It is the eyes which are the instrument
of conquest. To maintain the balance between the positive and
negative results of this love (or rather to tip the scales in favour
of the positive while not denying its negative aspects), the eyes are
first eulogised. Four epithets, all positive, by their position and
arrangement before the noun *regard,* form a gradation which cul-
minates in *divin* and also places the noun at the rhyme, thereby
giving it special emphasis within the structure of the line. The
*regard* is the instrument of Love's triumph and is described both
in terms of fire (*feu* and *ard*) and of penetration (*aiguillonne*). The
metaphor of fire is predominant, as two vehicles for it are used in
one line and as the verb *ard* is in the rhyming position and echoes
the first A rhyme *regard,* which suggests that fire is an integral
part of the eyes' nature:

> Le sage, doux, cher et divin regard,
> Duquel on fit de mon cueur la conqueste,
> Lorsqu'enyvré j'osay dresser la teste
> Pour voir le feu qui m'aiguillonne et ard,

After this extensive amplification of the *regard,* its contradictory
influences on the Lover are then catalogued in a series of antitheses
whose separate terms are delineated by "ores ... tout à coup" and
"ores ... ores." While the *regard* is not explicitly mentioned in the
second quatrain, its presence is implicit throughout the poem, as
every contradictory action and mood of the speaker is predicated
upon the action of the Beloved's eyes: it is the *regard* which "me
fait sembler ores un leopard" as well as all the other things enu-
merated in the second quatrain and the first tercet:

> Me fait sembler ores un leopard,
> Qui agité de fureur ne s'arreste,
> Puis tout à coup une craintive beste,
> Qui de son creux de tout le jour ne part.
>   Ore je suis un second Democrite,
> Ores la mort j'ay en ma face escrite,
> Or' le vermeil qui embellit les fleurs.
>   Ore en plaisir, ore en melancolie,
> Libre, & captif, me destache & relie,
> Baignant ses raiz dans la mer de mes pleurs.

It is also "le [...] divin regard" which is the elliptic subject of the sentence comprising the final tercet and it is here that we return to the fire imagery associated with the eyes in the first quatrain. The importance attributed to fire now assumes another dimension, for, in the sonnet's closing line, it becomes obvious that an implicit metaphor underpins the images of fire: the metaphor of the eye as sun. We also meet with the fire/eye/heart/eye/water progression we have noticed previously, for, as the final paradox of the poem, the beneficial rays of the sun-eye mingle with the hyperbolic sea of the Lover's tears, provoked by the sufferings of love, so that the two elemental antagonists, fire and water, are united by the power of the Beloved's gaze.

While lacking the poetic mastery of Labé or Du Guillet, Magny, despite an occasional lapse, does give the eyes the same kind of prominence in his poetry as his contemporary poetesses. The reader can certainly find fault with Magny's too frequent recourse to Petrarchan clichés which are not always reworked to fit into their new poetic context and so do not have the "original" and "personal" character we associate with Du Guillet, Labé or Scève. However, there are occasions when Magny does succeed in rejuvenating hackneyed material and despite its weaknesses, his use of eye imagery is certainly of more than historical interest.

### Pontus de Tyard

The eyes play an important and pervasive role in the poetry of Pontus de Tyard, although his use of eye imagery and of the aggressive eye topos tends to be less varied and more conventional than in the poets whose works we have already examined. The same elements are present in his work but Pontus often fails to exploit them fully and repeats images without introducing significant variations on his basic theme. The overall result is that eye imagery appears in his work more as a rhetorical ornament and convention than as a vital part of his exploration of the love experience. While convention is of course a factor in the works of all the poets of the Lyonese group, they usually succeed in integrating eye imagery into the metaphorical structure of their poetry in a much more coherent and satisfactory way than does Pontus.

The eyes usually figure prominently in the descriptions of the Beloved which abound in Pontus' love verse. In a "Chant a son

Leut," which is in fact a thinly disguised pretext for a *descriptio*,
we find the following portrait of the Lady's eyes and eyebrows, in
which the brows are implicitly compared to Cupid's bow and the
eyes to the sun:

> Chante ces arcs, souz lesquels Amour passe
> Quand sa douceur benine, ou rigueur fiere,
> De vie ou mort m'asseure, ou me menace.
>    Chante la grave et modeste maniere
> De ces beaux yeux, que le Soleil honore,
> Comme allumant son feu en leur lumiere. [37]

Similar in technique is the ode "Au ciel, en faveur de sa Dame."
Here, the Lover addresses a prayer to Heaven that his Lady, who
is a divinity and whose realm is therefore the sky, will look benignly
upon her worshipper. The first mention of the topos comes when
Heaven is personified as having eyes, which the Lover asks to dart
their beneficial rays upon his Lady. Here the organs of vision, while
not instruments for inspiring love, do have an analogous role in the
transmission of happiness:

> Et beninement luy riz
> De tes yeux plus favoriz,
>       Dont l'heur à ceux tu dardes
>       Que tu regardes.

Subsequently, the parallels between the eyes of Heaven and those
of the Beloved are exploited by the poet, and in a prayer the Lover
asks that the Lady emulate the sky's previous action by favouring
him with her glance. As a means of stressing the relationship between the Lady and the Heavens, her eyes are described, in a highly
conventional metaphor, as stars which are responsible for having
snatched away the Lover's life (aggressive attackers once again).
Further, the eyebrows are depicted as bows which shoot arrows
bearing death, or life if they are accompanied by *douceur* (that is,
the promise of reciprocity in love).

> Fais que ses lampegeans yeux,
> Ces deux Astres gracieux,

---

[37] Tyard, *Livre de vers lyriques* in Schmidt, op. cit., p. 375.

> Rendent l'ame à ma vie,
>   Qu'ils ont ravie.
> Et que ces arcs hebenins,
> Fais piteusement benins,
>   Les trets sur moy ne tirent,
>   Dont ils m'occirent.
> Mais qu'un tret de leur douceur,
> Descoché dedans mon cœur,
>   Jusques à l'ame pousse
>   La mort plus douce. [38]

In spite of the hackneyed use of traditional imagery, Tyard does stress the element of combat and strife in love more than most of the Lyonese poets (with the possible exceptions of Scève and Labé). The aggressive eye topos is exploited not simply to show the sudden and irresistible nature of the *innamoramento,* or the passivity of the Lover, victim of the aggressivity of the Love Object. Tyard links the topos more particularly to the love-as-war theme, which is certainly common enough in love poetry both during and before the Renaissance (Chrétien de Troyes is but one noteworthy example from the French Middle Ages). [39] However it is usually held separate from the aggressive eye topos itself (although the latter's arrows, darts and swords which pierce and wound obviously invite parallels between the two domains), whereas Tyard exploits it to underline his presentation of love as being primarily a state of strife and warfare.

The eyes are represented both as Cupid's lair and as his weapon in an interesting Epigramme. [40] Here the eyes do not shoot forth arrows but are a source of fire which Cupid uses to ignite the flame of love in the Beholder's heart. By a skilful use of *correctio* in the second line, the poet identifies the Lady's eyes both as sources of light and as heavenly bodies by referring to them metaphorically as *soleilz luisants.* In this way a parallel relationship between the eyes and fire is implicitly established, to be finally fused in an encompassing metaphor in the last line of the poem:

---

[38] Ibid., p. 377.
[39] Eugene Vance, "Le combat érotique chez Chrétien de Troyes," *Poétique,* 12, 1972.
[40] Tyard, *Les Erreurs,* op. cit., p. 101.

Un jour Amour voltigeoit dens tes yeux,
Ou bien plustot en tes soleilz luisans:
Pour estre en bref sur moy victorieux
Il allumoit quelques flambeaux cuisans:
   Et nous estions ensemble devisans,
Où ta douceur ravissoit tant mon ame
Que ce pendant avec ardente flame
Amour surprint mon cœur à l'impourveue:
   Lors m'embrasa du feu qui tant m'enflame,
Prins au brasier de ta brulante veue.

At first, the eyes and fire are held separate, as it is Cupid who is the principal actor in this comedy, although his partnership with the eyes is already made clear in the first line: "Un jour Amour voltigeoit dans tes yeux." Cupid himself then becomes a fire-bearer as he lights several torches in order to inflame the Lover's heart (the source of this fire is not immediately evident). In the second quatrain of the epigramme, a parallel assault on the Lover is undertaken by both the Beloved and Cupid. In the Beloved's case, it is her "douceur" which ravishes the Lover's soul while Cupid takes his heart by surprise with his flame. It is only in the last two lines of the poem that the collusion between the two aggressors is made quite clear, when it is stated that the source of Cupid's fire is in fact the Lady's eyes. This is expressed in a concise image which binds together the various parallels previously established between the Beloved and Cupid into one encompassing metaphor: "au brasier de ta brulante veue."

The same metaphor of the eyes as both sun and the fire of passion is developed even more fully in a *Sextine* (#35 in McClelland's edition). Here the power of the Lady's glance is compared to the warmth of the sun at the hottest period of the year:

Le plus ardent de tous les elemens
N'est si bouillant alors que le Soleil
Au fort d'esté le fier Lyon enflame,
Comme je sens aux doux traitz de ton œil
Estre enflamé et bouillante mon ame,
Le triste corps languissant en tormens.

Once again it is the eye which casts arrows (*traits*) and the same words (*bouillant* and *enflamer*) are used to refer to the effects of both the sun and the eye. The parallel action of the eye and the sun is further stressed in the next stanza, for like the sun, the eye inflames the Lover. As in the Epigramme which we have previously examined, Cupid is associated with the eyes' action, particularly with respect to fire, and the verb *enflamer,* previously used to describe the actions of both eye and sun is now applied to Cupid. His arrows are *cuisans* (compare *flambeaux cuisans* in the Epigramme) and the Lady's eye is "ton flamboyant œil" (compare "ta brulante veue" to be found in the Epigramme). The suffering caused by this intense heat produces tears, so that once more two antithetical and inimical elements, fire and water, find a paradoxical unity in the love relationship through the medium of the eye thanks to the organ of vision's association with both of them.

> Je voy souvent Amour lequel enflame
> Pour me donner plus gracieux tormens
> Ses traitz cuisans en ton flamboyant œil:
> Lors me muant en deux purs elemens,
> Le corps se fond en pleurs quand ce Soleil
> Empraint le feu plus ardemment en l'ame.

However, as is usually the case in Renaissance poetry, love has two faces and brings not merely suffering but also consolation. In an almost evangelical apostrophe to those whose souls are tormented by passion, the poet proposes the curative power of his Beloved's glance as a remedy for their tears. Here the rays of his sun will not burn as before, they will instead dry the tears. In addition, the *traitz* are no longer *cuisans,* as in stanza 3, but *doux* as at the beginning of the poem:

> Vienne secher toute langoureuse ame
> (Si comme moy Amour trop fort l'enflame)
> Ses tristes pleurs aux rays de mon Soleil.
> Vienne celuy qui comblé de tormens
> Se pleint de Dieu, du Ciel, des Elemens,
> Chercher confort au doux trait de cest œil.

The paradoxical nature of the eyes is then dealt with in the following stanza, where they send out both a *doux regard* and a *fier trait,* which make the soul either joyous or sorrowful respectively. The cosmic influence exerted by the eye over the Lover's soul is further reinforced by its effects on the elements and is reasserted by the mention of the total control which the eye-sun exercises over the emotional environment of the Lover's soul. It is the eye which brings heat or cold, light or darkness:

> Le doux regard du fier trait de cest œil
> Fait ou joyeuse ou dolente toute ame,
> Et temperez ou non les elemens:
> Aussi c'est luy qui rend froide ou enflame
> L'occasion de tous ces miens tormens,
> Et qui m'est nuict obscure ou clair Soleil.

The last two stanzas of the poem are but laboured variations on this theme and the syntactical and grammatical obscurity of the closing lines unfortunately diminishes the total poetic effect of this *Sextine de l'œil.*

In sonnet 36 [41] Tyard returns to his favourite use of the aggressive eye topos to present the aggression of Cupid upon the hapless Lover through the weapon of the Lady's eyes and eyebrows. After using the metaphor of hair as net to trap the Lover, Tyard in the second quatrain takes up the comparison of the Lady's eyebrows to Cupid's bow:

> Puis de tes yeux couvers et decorez
> D'un sourcil double en hebene noircy,
> Dont fit son arc d'ivoyre racourcy,
> Tira des traitz mortellement ferrez.

Having laid an ambush for the Lover whose own eyes attract him irresistibly to contemplate the beauty of the Lady's countenance, the trap is sprung in the second tercet, the attack takes place and Cupid uses the arrows of the Lady's eyes and bow of her brow to assault the helpless victim. We encounter in this tercet what might be described as a Renaissance counterpart to the modern concept of military "overkill" as Cupid bombards the Lover with arrows:

> Puis enfonçant son arc il descocha
> Tant de ses traitz sur moy qu'il se fascha
> De plus m'occire, et moy de plus mourir.

---

[41] Ibid., p. 134.

The ambush motif is taken up again in Sonnet 49 where the Lover's own eyes are explicitly blamed for his suffering and become, if not traitors, at least "mal cauts" and must bear the full responsibility for allowing Cupid, lurking in the Lady's eyes, entry into the citadel of his heart. It is not the gods or destiny who are responsible:'

> . . .
> Mais mon ennuy vient de vous seuls, mes yeux,
> Quand trop hardis vous vistes ma Deesse.
>  Amour estoit ce jour caché dedens
> Ces deux beaux yeux, ou bien soleils ardens,
> Desquelz mal cauts soustintes les regards.
>  Lors le cruel par vous au cœur passa,
> Et tant de fois de ses traitz le blessa
> Qu'encor de mal je pleins, je pleure et ars. [42]

The same use of the topos in, alas, much the same words is found once again in the Second Part of the *Erreurs amoureuses* in the fourth stanza of *Chanson 8:* [43]

> Le trait par vous, ô mes yeux, fut receu,
> Lequel blessa mon cueur si durement
> Quand, attirez d'un vain contentement,
>  Luy fistes ouverture.
> La, si par vous, mal cauts, je feuz deceu,
>  Vous en payez l'usure.

In De Tyard's verse, there are many other references to the eyes, references which attest to the importance he attributes to their role in the love experience. However, to examine them in greater detail would be tedious and unnecessary, since his subsequent use of the aggressive eye topos is largely repetitive and contains few of the variations we found in the other Lyonese poets.

A final word is in order, for if De Tyard was unable to exploit in depth the poetic possibilities of the topos, he was at least able to explore the full range of its psychological and physiological ramifications in a Neoplatonic-Petrarchan concept of the love experience and in this respect his work is worthy of interest.

---

[42] Ibid., p. 147.
[43] Ibid., p. 198.

As we turn now to Scève's use of the same material, we shall see just how much poetic richness can be extracted from this particular vein of imagery. Pontus de Tyard's verse with its unimaginative, pedestrian and repetitious use of the aggressive eye topos is a perfect foil to the subtlety and complexity which characterise Scève's treatment of eye imagery. While the components are basically the same, Scève almost always manages to rejuvenate conventional imagery in a way that Tyard seems unable to do, so that the topos becomes an exciting and constantly variegated foundation on which his eye imagery is constructed. In Scève's work, as in that of Labé and Du Guillet, there are many recapitulations of the basic metaphors associated with the topos but they are almost never simple repetitions, for each recapitulation and variation illuminates a new aspect of the type of eye imagery we have been examining. There is no "original" (in the modern sense) imagery in Renaissance poetry, for none was sought, desired or even imagined. What does give Renaissance poets their individuality (or lack of it) is their ability (or inability) to present traditional material in new ways and in new combinations. Du Guillet, Labé and Scève do this superbly, whereas Magny and Tyard only manage to do so sporadically. Our modern preference for the first three poets is not simply a question of changed tastes but comes from the much greater flexibility and sophistication of their poetic genius.

# CHAPTER III

## SCÈVE'S USE OF THE AGGRESSIVE EYE TOPOS

> Que ne suis donc, plus qu'Argus, tout en yeux?
> (*Délie*, CCXC)

THE ITINERARY of love traced by Maurice Scève in the *Délie* is inextricably linked to the power of the Beloved's glance. Indeed, of all the Lyonese poets, none makes as frequent and extensive use of the aggressive eye topos and its associated imagery as Scève. Love is not only initiated by the Beloved's gaze but is continuously being rejuvenated from this potent source, so that the *innamoramento,* which is the subject of the opening dizain, is also central to numerous other dizains scattered throughout the *Délie* and becomes itself one of the poem's leitmotifs. The constant return to the birth of love in the Beholder's soul results in a perpetual reactualisation of this privileged moment and a reaffirming of the eyes' primordial role in the love experience. Hans Staub, in his perceptive study of Scève's poetry,[1] has stressed the importance of the eyes in *Délie:*

> Scève est d'abord poète du regard; il le sera d'un bout à l'autre de ce recueil qui commence par le mot *l'Oeil.*

Indeed, a careful reading of the *Délie* suggests that the traditional interpretation of its title as an anagramme for *l'Idée* may be worth retaining after all, provided that the word is understood not so much in terms of pure Neo-Platonism but rather as a derivation

---

[1] Hans Staub, *Le Curieux désir* (Geneva: Droz, 1967), p. 37.

from the Greek *idein,* meaning "to see." Délie would then combine in her person not only the attributes of the moongoddess trinity (the celestial and terrestrial Diana together with Hecate): she would also be, and perhaps primarily so, "she who is seen." [2]

Scève's fascination, one could even say obsession, with the power of the eyes to inspire love (when it is a question of the Beloved's eyes) or to admit the baleful glance (in the case of the Lover), is present whenever love is the subject of his poetry. Already in 1536, well before the *Délie* (1544), we find that the eyes are central to his rhetoric of love. This was the year when the young humanist, already known as the discoverer of Laure de Nove's supposed tomb in Avignon, was caught up in another of the literary vogues of his time, that of the *blasons du corps féminin.* [3] Instituted by Marot during his exile at Ferrara, the *blason* became, temporarily at least, the favourite genre of the French Renaissance poets of the thirties and culminated in the famous *Concours des blasons,* from which Scève emerged victorious with his *Blason du sourcil:*

> Sourcil tractif en vouste fleschissant
> Trop plus qu'hebene, ou jayet noircissant,
> Hault forgeté pour umbrager les yeulx,
> Quand ils font signe, ou de mort ou de mieulx,
> Sourcil qui rend paoureux les plus hardis,
> Et courageux les plus accouardis,
> Sourcil qui faict l'air clair, obscur soubdain,
> Quand il froncist par yre, ou par desdain,
> Et puis le rend serain, clair et joyeulx,
> Quand il est doulx, plaisant et gratieux,
> Sourcil qui chasse et provoque les nues
> Selon que sont ses archées tenues,
> Sourcil assis au lieu hault pour enseigne,
> Par qui le cueur son vouloir nous enseigne,
> Nous descouvrant sa profunde pensée,

---

[2] Another interpretation of the title, which has not been previously suggested, involves a different anagramme formed from the word Délie. Délie is also the anagramme of Elide, the French form of Elis, the Greek province conquered by Endymion, with whom Artemis/Diana/Delia subsequently fell in love. The poet in fact identifies himself with Endymion in Dizain 127 and the association of Délie and Elide would indicate the poet-lover's desire for reciprocity, together with his despair that reciprocity in love will never be forthcoming in this life. See for additonal connotations of the title, François Rigolot's *Poétique et onomastique,* Geneva, 1977, pp. 105-126.

[3] See Albert-Marie Schmidt, *Poètes du XVIè siècle* (Paris, 1969).

Ou soit de paix, ou de guerre offensée,
Sourcil non pas sourcil, mais ung soubz ciel
Qu'est le dixiesme et superficiel,
Où l'on peult veoir deux estoilles ardantes,
Lesquelles sont de son arc dependantes,
Estincelans plus souvent et plus clair
Qu'en esté chault ung bien soubdain esclair;
Sourcil qui faict mon espoir prosperer,
Et tout à coup me faict desesperer;
Sourcil sus qui amour prit le pourtraict
Et le patron de son arc qui attraict
Hommes et Dieux à son obeissance,
Par triste Mort, ou doulce jouyssance,
O sourcil brun, soubz tes noires tenebres
J'ensepvely en desirs trop funebres
Ma liberté et ma dolente vie,
Qui doulcement par toy me fut ravie. [4]

This poem is as much a *blason du regard* as it is of the eyebrow, since the latter assumes the properties of the eye, due to their anatomical proximity in the geography of the Beloved's face. The poem begins with an architectural metaphor, which gives a monumental and haughty quality to the eye-brow. By stressing its extreme blackness with two nouns denoting substances which are in fact synonymous with that colour, Scève adds to his description of the Lady's brow a dark funereal connotation which he will develop later in the poem. It is in line three that the close relationship (a relationship which in this poem amounts to interchangeability of role) between the eye and the eye-brow becomes explicit, for the lofty position of the latter is explained by its function which is to "umbrager les yeulx." In turn the eyes are associated with the blackness attributed to the eyebrows through the verb *umbrager*. Once this link between the two has been affirmed, the poet evokes the tyranny which the eyes exercise over the Lover and the eyebrow is implicitly associated with this dominion, as the eyes "font signe

---

[4] Maurice Scève, *Œuvres complètes,* ed. Pascal Quignard (Paris: Mercure de France, 1974), pp. 363-364. This is the latest edition of Scève's works and has the advantage of comprising all of Scève's works, both prose and poetry. As far as the *Délie* is concerned however, its usefulness is limited since, incomprehensibly, it does not reproduce the emblems. It is also deficient in critical apparatus. When quoting from the *Délie,* we will use McFarlane's excellent edition.

de mort ou de mieulx." The "mort" refers, of course, to the state of the Lover when the Beloved's gaze indicates rejection, the *mieulx* signifies his happiness when her eyes regard him with favour. The parallelism of functions is further strengthened when, immediately after the eyes' influence is described in terms of this life and death antithesis, a similar power is attributed to the *sourcil*. This co-alescence is reinforced on the stylistic level by the use of a series of double antitheses to characterise the effects produced by the eyebrows: not only does the eyebrow "rend paoureux les plus hardis," but it also makes "courageux les plus accouardis," depend-ing (and this is implicit) on whether the eyes have signaled either *mort* or *mieulx*. The Lover's psychological state is totally dependent on the eyes and their appendages, and such is their power that they can totally transform the character of the Lover at will. However, the eyes and their attendant brows exercise their sway not only over the microcosm of the Lover but also over the macrocosm itself. Since the universe of the poem is a universe totally dominated by love, the macrocosm appears as a reflection of the Lover's micro-cosm and is influenced in the same way by love's message as trans-mitted by the eyebrows. Thus a sign from the *sourcil* affects the atmosphere just as it influences the Lover's state of mind. It makes "l'air clair, obscur soubdain" when it frowns "par yre ou par des-dain," and as the double antithetical pattern is pursued, the air becomes "serein, clair et joyeux" when the eyebrow is "doulx, plaisant et gracieux." We have in fact almost a prefiguration of the pathetic fallacy, as Nature's response to the movement of the Lady's brow is directly parallel to the Lover's inner state. There is of course an important difference — the universe only appears to mir-ror the Lover's feelings. It is in fact directly affected not by him but by the god-like power of Délie. All elements of the natural world are equally subject to her influence.

In his *blason,* Scève transfers another of the commonplaces usually associated with the eyes to the eyebrows. Whereas usually it is the eyes which are called the mirror of the soul, here it is the eyebrows which reflect the feelings of the Beloved's heart "nous descouvrant sa profonde pensée / Ou soit de paix ou de guerre offensée," and their basic aggressiveness is clearly underlined in the military metaphor upon which the antithesis is based.

Precisely at the mid-point of the poem, the imagery associates the eyebrows not only with terrestrial natural phenomena but with celestial forces as well. If the eyebrows have thus far been godlike in the power they wield over the Lover and his natural environment, in line 17 they are explicitly identified with the driving force of the whole universe in a grandiose treatment of the "Love makes the world go round" theme. Playing on the phonetic similarity between "sourcil" and "sous-ciel," [5] the poet associates the eyebrow with the tenth heaven of Renaissance cosmology ("[...] mais un sous-ciel / Qu'est le dixiesme et superficiel"), that is the Primum Mobile which is the highest heaven of all, which is "superficial" because it is at the surface of a spherical universe of which the earth is both the centre and the lowest point, and which is next to the empyrean, the habitat of God. From this lofty realm shine the two stars which are dependent on the eyebrows' arch, and this image associates the eyes both with the divine and with the astrological influence which Renaissance men believed the stars exercised over them.

After such an ascension to the pinnacle of the universe, the eyes themselves initiate a downward movement into the terrestrial world when they are identified with summer lightning. This return from an outer space far-removed from sublunar contradictions reinstates the antithetical pattern associated with the eyebrows' workings. They now successively encourage hope or suddenly plunge the Lover into despair. The coupling of these two opposite states, which are unified in the ambivalent experience of love, is reinforced by the *rime riche*: "prosperer/desesperer," in which the common sound "-sperer" evokes the verb "espérer," already suggested by the presence of the noun *espoir.*

In the final six lines of the *blason,* the poet completes a magnificent circular sweep which associates the imagery of this section with the first antithesis used to describe the effect the eyebrows have on the Lover ("mort/mieulx"). Here, in a traditional comparison which has acquired new meaning after the previous soaring of the eyebrows into the realm of the divine, the eyebrows become

---

[5] It is important to remember that for the Renaissance poet, this is not gratuitous word-play. It was part of poetic doctrine that language is a veil which covers hidden truth and that the artisan of language — the poet — is able to lift this veil.

the model for the bow of the God of Love. Since Eros holds sway over both men and gods, the eyebrows share this ultimate sovereignty, for they bring either "triste mort" or "doulce jouissance." Here the "mort/mieulx" pair of line four has been appropriately amplified by the addition of an adjective to each noun and the use of the more precise "jouissance" instead of the rather vague "mieulx," whose initial consonant connected it by alliteration to "mort." However, the final image evokes the death of the Lover, as the eyebrows become a source of intense darkness ("noires tenebres"), burying the speaker's freedom and very life in funereal desires. Yet as the verb "ensepvely" is both active and in the first person, the effect is not a totally negative one, for the verb suggests a voluntary surrender on the part of the Lover. The positive aspect of the sacrifice is affirmed in the closing line of the poem where the ravishing of the Lover is coupled with the adverb "doulcement," which recalls the "doulx" of line ten and the "doulce jouissance" of line twenty eight. The fact that the final lines return to images of darkness after the imagery has passed through the light of the heavenly realms is also symbolic of the carnal aspect of the speaker's love experience. This is an important theme in the Délie, as we shall see, [6] and in this respect too, the Blason du sourcil announces the principal aspects of the eye imagery we find in the Délie. The sourcil is after all a metonymy for the eye and all the characteristics attributed to the eyebrow in this blason are those of the eyes.

If the eyes already figure prominently in the description of love prior to 1544 in Scève's poetry, their role is even more important in the Délie. So large is the number of references to the part they play in engendering and sustaining love there, that it becomes necessary to divide them into categories in order to do justice to the richness and density of the motif. Whenever several of these categories overlap or are used side by side in the same poem, they will be dealt with together to avoid having to violate the unity of individual dizains and isolating images from their poetic context, since our principal interest is in the poetic dynamics of the aggressive eye topos and not in the establishment of a catalogue.

---

[6] See Henri Wéber's illuminating discussion of Scève's poetry in La création poétique au XVIè siècle en France (Paris: Nizet, 1956), pp. 161-230.

The somewhat arbitrary but necessary divisions we have chosen are the following:

1) the eye as weapon (which is by far the largest category and which includes any reference, explicit or implicit, to the eye as wounding, piercing or causing physical harm to the recipient of its gaze);

2) the eye as a source of poison or venom;

3) the eye as a source of and a dispenser of fire;

4) the eye as a lightning flash (which is an intermediate category between 3 and 5);

5) the eye as star or sun (or any source of bright light that implies identification with stellar radiance, which means that references to *clarté* will fall under this category);

6) the eye as moon (lunar light, while obviously associated with other kinds of light, is nonetheless a separate entity in view of Délie's association with the Moon Goddess).

## 1) *The Eye as Weapon*

> L'Œil trop ardent en mes jeunes erreurs
> Girouettoit, mal cault, a l'impourveue:
> Voicy (ô paour d'agreables terreurs)
> Mon Basilisque avec sa poingnant' veue
> Perçant Corps, Cœur, & Raison despourveue,
> Vint penetrer en l'Ame de mon Ame.
>   Grand fut le coup, qui sans tranchante lame
> Fait, que vivant le Corps, l'Esprit desvie,
> Piteuse hostie au conspect de toy, Dame,
> Constituée Idole de ma vie.

If our preliminary study of the *Blason du sourcil* did not convince us of the great importance Scève attributes to the eyes and their gaze, the first dizain of the *Délie* should immediately dispel any lingering doubts, thanks to its stark beginning which, by placing

---

[7] As already stated, all poems from the *Délie* are quoted from I. D. Mc-Farlane, *Maurice Scève: Délie* (Cambridge, 1966). We have, however, taken the liberty of slightly modifying McFarlane's spellings by using "j" for "i," "v" for "u" (so that his *ieunes erreurs* becomes *jeunes* and his *impourueue* becomes *impourveue*). These spellings appear to be a vagary of Scève's printers and do not correspond to normal sixteenth century usage. Pascal Quignard has adopted this principle also in his edition of Scève.

the word *l'Oeil* at the head of the first poetic unit of the work, establishes it as a portal to the whole *canzoniere*. "L'Œil trop ardent" both introduces and encompasses the poet's persona, whom this synecdoche reduces to pure gaze. The singularity of his purpose is at once evident in the singular of the grammatical form. The choice of *l'œil* rather than *les yeux* indicates that what is important is not so much the eyes as physical organs but the eye as *regard,* seeking out and attempting to "reprendre sous garde" [8] what lies beyond its corporal limits. However, this same movement towards the exterior causes the *regard* to isolate itself, so that it becomes vulnerable to external forces and influences. It is ironic that the Lover's eye, in its search for what is primarily erotic domination (this connotation is clearly suggested by the expressions "trop ardent" and "jeunes erreurs"), itself falls victim to the purposeful gaze of the Other. As Jean Starobinski has pointed out, [9] "voir est un acte dangereux" and the eye's random scanning (suggested both by the verb "girouettoit" and by the identification of "erreurs" not only with "error" but also with "errare," to wander) [10] is countered by the steadfastness of Délie's basilisk glance. In this case, the Other's glance is not only aggressive but is as deadly as a lethal weapon. Firstly, it forces the Lover's wandering gaze to fix itself upon Délie's own eyes, thus creating in the Lover a new stability, which is stressed by the use of *Voicy* which contains the full force of its etymology: "Vois — ici." Délie's glance then actively penetrates all three parts of the Lover's microcosmic trinity (body, heart, reason) and the power of its penetration is clearly suggested by Scève's use of three alliterative synonyms: *poingnant, perçant* and *penetrer* to describe the progressive inward movement of Délie's glance. This active verbal trinity associated with the Lady's eyes overwhelms the three nouns referring to the Lover, which are helplessly clustered together in the centre of line five and are thus at the geometric centre of the dizain. The sword-like sharpness of the Beloved's glance and its lethal potential is further accentuated by the expression Scève uses to describe the innermost recesses of the Lover's being, a phrase directly inspired by Leone

---

[8] See Jean Starobinski, *L'Œil vivant* (Paris, 1961), p. 11.
[9] Ibid., p. 14.
[10] See Jacqueline Risset, *Délie ou l'anagramme du désir* (Rome: Mario Bulzini, 1971).

Ebreo: [11] "l'ame de mon ame". Scève extracts the symbolic possibilities of this expression by a play on words. In French, "l'ame de mon ame" can be not only a metaphysical concept (meaning "soul of my soul"), it also suggests its homophone "lame de mon ame," "lame" denoting in sixteenth century French both "blade" and "tombstone." All three readings are apt descriptions of the effect of Délie's gaze on the Lover's soul and are reminiscent of her triple function as Moon Goddess (soul of my soul), Huntress (blade of my soul), and Underworld Deity (tombstone of my soul).

The final dissolution of the Lover's autonomy is accomplished in the second part of the dizain (where the rhyme word of line 7 is *lame* and echoes "l'ame de mon ame"), as he becomes a "piteuse hostie au conspect de toy" ("conspect" from "conspicio" meaning to look at attentively). The great paradox of this experience is that the *innamoramento* brings at once death and life. If the rays transmitted by Délie's eyes wound mortally, they also bring subsequent resurrection for the Beloved is now "l'Idole de ma vie," installed in the inner sanctum of the Lover's being as a perpetual object of contemplation. As Hans Staub has remarked, the original egotistical centre around which the Lover's eye formerly gravitated, has now been abolished and a new centre constituted. [12]

This passage through death to a new life and its relationship to the Beloved's gaze is forcefully demonstrated in the last four lines of the sizain by the rhymes *desvie* ("die") and *vie*. Just as in lines two and five the rhyme words *impourveue* and *despourveue* contain the *veue* of line four, so *desvie* contains its opposite: *vie*. Neither is it coincidental that *veue* and *vie* are near homophones, with the result that *veue* announces *desvie* but ultimately restores *vie*. The trajectory and effects of Délie's fatal yet beneficial glance are in this way reaffirmed at the level of the poem's rhymes.

Dizain 5 (the last of the introductory group of five) also deals with Délie's wounding glance; however in this poem the treatment of the topos is more conventional and treats only the negative aspect of the effects of the Beloved's gaze:

---

[11] Leone Ebreo, *Dialoghi d'amore,* ed. Santino Caramella (Bari, 1929), p. 177: "La mente spirituale (che è cuore di nostro cuore e anima di nostra anima [...])."

[12] Staub, op. cit., p. 37.

Ma Dame ayant l'arc d'Amour en son poing
Tiroit a moy, pour a soy m'attirer:
Mais je gaignay aux piedz, & de si loing,
Qu'elle ne sceut oncques droit me tirer.
   Dont me voyant sain, & sauf retirer,
Sans avoir faict a mon corps quelque bresche:
Tourne, dit elle, a moy, & te despesche.
Fuys tu mon arc, ou puissance, qu'il aye?
   Je ne fuys point, dy je, l'arc ne la flesche:
Mais l'œil, qui feit a mon cœur si grand' playe.

The power of Délie's eyes is established within the framework of a hunting metaphor, in which Délie is implicitly identified with the huntress Diana and the Lover becomes her hapless victim who is attempting to escape from her dominion over him. Like Diana, Délie carries a bow and arrows, but unlike that of her mythological counterpart, this bow becomes, like everything in Scève's love-oriented univers, "l'arc d'Amour," which immediately places the Lover's flight and subsequent conversation on a metaphorical and allegorical level. The attraction Délie exercises over the Lover is underlined by the use of internal rhyme and homophony in line two where we find: *tiroit* and *attirer, a moy* and *a soy,* "tiroit à *moy*" and "*m*'attirer." In spite of this impressive rhetorical arsenal used to describe Délie's actions, the Lover seems at first to have got the better of his pursuer and to have escaped from her power. The victory is more apparent than real however, as it takes only a word from the Lady to stop his retreat. It is in the subsequent conversation that the bow of love proves to be less powerful than that other dispenser of arrows, Délie's eyes. This potent weapon constitutes the real danger, since the bow in Délie's hand can harm only the body ("Sans avoir faict à mon corps quelque breche"), whereas her gaze penetrates right to his heart. However, the Lover's knowledge of the danger inherent in Délie's gaze has come too late to be a defense against its effects, since, as we learn in the last line of the dizain, her eyes have already done their work (the past definite *feit* is used to describe their action on the Lover's heart). Chronologically then, we are situated *post factum* and the Lover's flight comes too late to save him. In fact, in one sense the whole dizain is a rhetorical construct, whose purpose is to amplify the overwhelming power of Délie's eyes, for since the mention of Cupid's bow in line one immediately conjures up the whole mytho-

logical background of Cupid's victories over men and gods alike,
the Lover's impotence here only serves to enhance the potency of
Délie's glance.

Dizain 6 is the first poem to recapitulate the *innamoramento*
which was the subject of Dizain 1. Like the latter, it is also a
"first" in the *Délie,* being the first of the forty-nine groups of nine
dizains (49 × 9) into which all but the first five and the last three
poetic units of the work are divided. It is also the first dizain to
be preceded by an engraved emblem, depicting in this case the
curiously ambiguous symbol of a wounded unicorn with its head
on the lap of a woman. Usually associated with chastity and hence,
by extension, with the Virgin, the unicorn here appears to represent
the wounded Lover, as evidenced by the motto "Pour le veoir je
pers la vie." This inclines McFarlane to state that the unicorn here
"symbolises the attraction and dangers of woman." [13] What is important from our point of view is the fact that the unicorn has
been wounded by what appears to be an arrow (the empennage is
the only part of the missile which is visible) and that the inflicting
of this wound is associated with the act of seeing in the motto:

> Libre vivois en l'Avril de mon aage,
> De cure exempt soubz celle adolescence,
> Ou l'œil, encor non expert de dommage,
> Se veit surpris de la doulce presence,
> Qui par sa haulte, & divine excellence
> M'estonna l'Ame, & le sens tellement,
> Que de ses yeulx l'archier tout bellement
> Ma liberté luy à toute asservie:
> Et des ce jour continuellement
> En sa beaulté gist ma mort, & ma vie.

Here many of the same elements we found in Dizain 1 are present,
except that the Lover's existence before the fatal event is not described in reprobative terms of excess (we find no "trop ardent,"
"jeunes erreurs" or "girouettoit"). The accent is on freedom and
youth: "Libre vivois en l'Avril de mon aage." Yet this freedom
is also presented as being in some sense negative and passive, since
no positive action is attributed to the Lover. He exists in an emotional and spiritual vacuum, much like that described in Du Guillet's

---

[13] McFarlane, op. cit., p. 123.

verse. He is simply "de cure exempt" and the eye is "non expert de dommage." Even the description of the *innamoramento* underlines the passivity of this youthful liberty, since the Lover's eye "*se* veit surpris." And yet this violation of his innermost person is accomplished with the co-operation of the victim himself, as the gaze is turned upon itself, as it sees itself being perceived and thus emerges into consciousness. Here the aggressor is the Beloved's gaze presented within the framework of the arrow imagery which is so often a part of the topos. The basic metaphor of Dizain 5 is here refined since the instrument of aggression and conquest is not the Lady herself but "de ses yeulx l'archier" (note that the plural is used for Délie's eyes, thus differentiating them from *l'œil* of the Lover). The adjective *Libre* which was the first word in this dizain, is recapitulated in noun form in line eight: "Ma liberté luy à toute asservie." Once more the loss of freedom and subsequent death/ life state are presented in a paradoxical light for the Lover is assaulted here, not by the frightening and diabolical basilisk of the first dizain, but by "la doulce presence," characterised by its "haulte & divine excellence." Similarly, the participle *asservie,* despite its negative connotations, contains the word *vie,* which was already suggested in line four by the use of its homophone, the past definite of *voir*: *se veit,* and finally reveals itself in the last line of the dizain as the rhyme for *asservie,* thus giving a positive closural effect to the poem. Just as in Dizain 1, *voir* and *vie* are again intimately connected and the ramifications of the aggressive eye's action are once more found at all levels of the poem's structure.

The lethal effects of the love glance are further explored in Dizain 16, which is, like Dizain 5, an amplification of the theme of the power of Délie's gaze:

> Je preferoys a tous Dieux ma Maistresse,
> Ainsi qu'Amour le m'avoit commandé:
> Mais la Mort fiere en eut telle tristesse,
> Que contre moy son dard à desbandé.
> Et quand je l'ay au besoing demandé
> Le m'à nyé, comme pernicieuse.
>    Pourquoy sur moy, ô trop officieuse,
> Pers tu ainsi ton povoir furieux?
> Veu qu'en mes mortz Delie ingenieuse
> Du premier jour m'occit de ses beaulx yeulx.

As in Dizain 5, Délie's superiority is affirmed as she is transformed into a deity to be worshipped above all other gods at the express command of the God of Love. This apparently unambiguous situation, which recalls the closing line of the first dizain, is complicated in line three by the appearance of another divine being, the Goddess of Death. Jealous of the exclusive power Délie exercises over the Lover, Death, whom he had asked to put an end to his sufferings, refuses him her services. This Goddess, whose ascendency is even more undisputed than is Love's, is unwilling or unable to overcome and nullify the power of Délie's eyes. They have already usurped Death's domain by bringing not simply the death which is the normal end of human existence, but repeated deaths ("mes mortz"), which are part of the Lover's paradoxical state. [14] Just as the arrows from Délie's eyes proved themselves to be more dangerous than those of Cupid's bow, so here Délie's fatal glance not only surpasses the power of Death but renders Death incapable of afflicting the Lover. Again we encounter the cycle sight-love-death and as before, in spite of the funereal tones of the dizain, the "deaths" wrought by Délie's eyes in the Lover's soul do in fact protect him from Death. As is implied by the plural *mortz,* each of the deaths inflicted by Délie results in a subsequent ressuscitation, since any form of death can occur only where life is first present, life and death being not contraries but corollaries.

Dizain 30 returns to the moment of the inception of Love but concentrates particularly on the internal physiological and psychological effects of the first love-glance:

> Des yeulx, ausquelz s'enniche le Soleil,
> Quand sus le soir du jour il se depart,
> Delasché fut le doulx traict nompareil
> Me penetrant jusques en celle part,
> Ou l'Ame attaincte or' a deux il despart,
> Laissant le cœur le moins interessé,
> Et toutesfois tellement oppressé,
> Que du remede il ne s'ose enquerir.
>    Car, se sentant quasi Serpent blessé,
> Rien ne le peult, non Dorion, guerir.

---

[14] As in the preliminary huitain of the *Délie* where Scève had written to introduce his poem: "Mais bien les mortz qu'en moy tu renouvelles / Je t'ay voulu en cest Oeuvre descrire."

Once again it is the Beloved's eyes which are the instruments of aggression and accordingly the word *yeulx,* in the opening line of the dizain, is strategically placed before the caesura, situated here at the end of the second foot. A moment of suspense is created as the action which will be performed by Délie's eyes is retarded by Scève's skilful manipulation of the poem's syntax. It is not until the eyes (and it is not clear until line three whether "*des* yeulx" is merely the partitive or the definite article combined with the preposition *de*) are endowed with cosmic significance, becoming the sun's residence, that the familiar arrow imagery appears as subject of the verb "delasché fut." At first it is devoid of negative overtones, thanks to the relationship established between the sun and Délie's eyes and to the fact that the word *traict* is cushioned by the two favourable adjectives *doulx* and *nompareil.* It is only when the arrow-like glance begins its penetration of the body and soul of the Lover that the ambivalent nature of the love-glance's aggression becomes apparent, as the soul is split in two. The ravaging progress of the glance reaches the heart, which is so oppressed that in the last two lines, it is identified with a wounded serpent, a particularly important identification within the framework of the *Délie*'s metaphorical system. In the opening dizain, Délie was equated with this normally masculine symbol, the mythical basilisk being considered in Antiquity and in the Renaissance as part of the snake family. Here the Lover shares the same symbol but with an essential difference: just as he was a wounded unicorn in the first emblem, here he is a wounded serpent, unable to cure its own injury. This is indeed a radical departure from the usual representation of the snake as an aggressive and dangerous animal for whose bite it is difficult or even impossible to find an antidote. In a sense, this reversal of roles, so frequent in the *Délie,* is anticipated when, in the opening lines of the dizain, the masculine symbol of the Sun is both associated with and subordinated to the Lady's eyes. Consequently their relationship is significant not only on a cosmological level (as a further demonstration of the parallels between macro- and microcosm) and philosophical level (the sun/eye brings spiritual knowledge and enlightenment), but also on an erotic level, for despite its Platonic overtones, the love Scève describes is threefold in nature, like Délie herself, and operates on an infernal as well as terrestrial and celestial plane.

Dizain 89, which as a loose translation of a Neo-Latin epigramme
by Jean Visagier,[15] is in a much more frivolous vein and yet at
the same time it does serve to further amplify Délie's superiority
over even the God of Love himself as well as to demonstrate the
ascendency of her glance:

> Amour perdit les traictz, qu'il me tira,
> Et de douleur se print fort a complaindre:
> Venus en eut pitié, & souspira,
> Tant que par pleurs son brandon feit esteindre,
> Dont aigrement furent contrainctz de plaindre:
> Car l'Archier fut sans traict, Cypris sans flamme.
>   Ne pleure plus, Venus: Mais bien enflamme
> Ta torche en moy, mon cœur l'allumera:
> Et toy, Enfant, cesse: va vers ma Dame,
> Qui de ses yeux tes flesches refera.

The tone is reminiscent of Dizain 5, where Délie was depicted as
firing arrows from Cupid's bow, arrows which failed to reach their
target. Here, Cupid himself is the marksman, who is unable to
wound the Lover. In fact he has unsuccessfully shot all his arrows
and has no more ammunition. The tears of chagrin he sheds extinguish Venus' flame, so that both deities of love are now deprived
of their usual attributes and powers. Here the Lover offers his help
and attests to the strength of his love by offering to rekindle
Venus' torch from his heart. In this instance, his love, since it was
inspired by Délie, is even more powerful than the Goddess of Love
and yet he is willing to offer her his assistance. He then advises
Cupid to go to his Lady, for her eyes will be able to refurbish him
with the arrows he needs. This affirms the pre-eminence of Délie,
while at the same time suggesting the Lover's willing acceptance
of his bitter-sweet fate, since, as the Lover well knows, Cupid will
use his refurbished weapons to wound the Lover again.

The mythological ramifications of Délie's eyes are further explored in Dizain 131, where Délie is compared to her namesake
Delia (Diana the huntress) to the latter's detriment:

> Delia ceincte, hault sa cotte attournée
> La trousse au col, & arc, & flesche aux mains,

---

[15] McFarlane, op. cit., pp. 396-7.

Exercitant chastement la journée,
Chasse, & prent cerfz, biches, & chevreulx maints.
   Mais toy, Delie, en actes plus humains
Mieulx composée, & sans violentz dardz,
Tu venes ceulx par tes chastes regardz,
Qui tellement de ta chasse s'ennuyent:
Qu'eulx tous estantz de toy sainctement ardz,
Te vont suyvant, ou les bestes la fuyent.

The first four lines of the dizain are the vehicle for a fairly standard iconographical portrayal of Delia/Diana at work hunting. The poet devotes the whole of line two to describing her weapons and of line four to detailing her success in her pastime. The link between these two lines, which deal with her attributes and achievements, is further stressed by the rhyme *mains/maints,* a homophonous monosyllabic word forming the rhyme in each case.

The next six lines of the dizain are clearly separated from the preceding quatrain by the initial *Mais,* as well as by the use of the second person pronoun *toy* (the description of Delia's activities having been given in the third person). In addition, Diana was designated by the latinised form of her name, Deli*a,* to further distinguish her from Délie in spite of the similarities between the two. Délie's transcendence over her mythological namesake is further emphasized by the poet's use of the comparatives *plus* and *mieulx.* The *plus* is attached to the adjective *humains* which, although it is associated by its rhyme with *mains* and *maints* is in contrast to them both semantically and by the fact it has two syllables as opposed to their monosyllabic form. Not only are Délie's acts more human, but she is "mieulx composée" and is without any weapons. Her hunting implements are her chaste glances which both link her to Delia (who occupied her day *chastement* in line three) and distinguish the unarmed huntress of men from the armed huntress of animals.

Délie's glances, while reminiscent of Delia since they are chaste, have another property which sets them apart from the mythological huntress' weapons. They transmit fire to those whom Délie pursues, so that her victims are burned with the fire of sacred love. They are so harrassed by her hunting that, in contrast to the beasts which flee from Diana's arrows, they willingly follow Délie who has instilled love's holy fire in them.

In spite of their superficial similarities as huntresses, in every other respect Delia and Délie are different and the whole poem is based on the series of subtly developed antitheses which establish Délie's clear superiority over her mythological sister, a superiority based once more on the irresistible power of her gaze. For if she is without *"violentz dardz"* here, she is not without *dardz,* as the rhyme *dardz/regardz* reminds us.

In Dizain 327, Scève pursues his reaffirmation of Délie's superiority by placing her in another semi-mythological framework and by showing that her power is greater even than that of the mythological deities.

> Delie aux champs troussée, & accoustrée
> Comme un Veneur, s'en alloit esbatant.
> Sur le chemin d'amour fut rencontrée,
> Qui par tout va jeunes Amantz guettant:
> Et luy à dit, près d'elle volletant:
> Comment? vas tu sans armes a la chasse?
>   N'ay je mes yeulx, dit elle, dont je chasse,
> Et par lesquelz j'ay maint gibbier surpris?
>   Que sert ton arc, qui rien ne te pourchasse,
> Veu mesmement que par eulx je t'ay pris?

As is Dizain 131, Délie is presented as a huntress, but rather than being contrasted to the mythological figure of Delia/Diana as before, she is here implicitly identified with the Goddess of the Hunt and her power is measured against that of Cupid, also a hunter of sorts, as he goes about with bow and arrow seeking his prey. In the opening lines, Délie is described as joyously frolicking in the fields in hunter's garb. That her excursion is not a gratuitous one is made clear in line three when she encounters Cupid, described periphrastically as "qui par tout va jeunes Amantz guettant." Although the Lover serves purely as narrator rather than narrator/actor in this poem, the expression "jeunes Amantz" recalls his own condition when he first perceived Délie ("jeunes erreurs," "livre vivois en l'Avril de mon aage"). What follows is not simply a testimony to Délie's amatory power but also a means of revenge on the God of Love who collaborated with Délie in his downfall. And if Délie represents spiritual love here, as is often the case, then her subjugation of Cupid is the victory of this love over the sensual love of the Wingèd Boy.

Cupid, who engages Délie in conversation, expresses surprise that she carries no hunting weapons in spite of her attire (this representation of her also harks back to Dizain 131 where she was "sans violentz dardz"). As before, her weapon is her eyes, which not only have surprised and wounded "maint gibbier" (as apposed to Cupid's bow which has procured him nothing at all), but have conquered the God of Love himself, so that the hunter has unwittingly become the hunted, all because of the invincible weapon which is Délie's gaze.

Dizain 140 also represents the power of Délie's eyes by a mythological code and makes use of a frequent element of the aggressive eye topos, that the Beloved's eyebrows are Cupid's bows.

> A Cupido je fis maintz traictz briser
> Sans que sur moy il peut avoir puissance,
> Et pour me vaincre il se va adviser
> De son arc mettre en ton obeissance:
>    Point ne faillit, & j'en euz congnoissance,
> Bien que pour lors fusse sans jugement.
> Et toutesfois j'apperçeuz clerement,
> Que tes sourcilz estoient d'Amour les arcz.
>    Car tu navras mon cœur trop asprement
> Par les longz traictz de tes perceanz regardz.

The dizain reworks the *innamoramento* theme in terms of the alliance between Cupid and Délie. The poem is divided into three sections, two quatrains and a couplet, corresponding to the three stages of the Lover's subjection. The first quatrain represents Cupid's repeated and ineffectual attacks on the Lover. Just as in Dizain 89, the *maintz traictz* aimed at the Lover do not wound their target and only serve to underline the Lover's superiority over Cupid, who, when acting alone, is powerless to vanquish his intended victim. The Lover's invulnerability to Cupid is in turn testimony to the Lady's own pre-eminence in the domain of love, since only an alliance of Cupid and Délie enables the former to gain dominion over the Lover: Cupid's bow is only effective when under her command.

The second quatrain briefly recapitulates the conquest of the Lover and here his former superiority is to no avail, for not only is he conquered, but he admits in line six that "bien que pour lors fusse sans jugement," a statement which recalls the negative pre-love state evoked in Dizain 6. Yet such is the power of Délie's glance that the Lover realises, in a sudden illumination, that Cupid is now using her glances as the arrows of love. The deadly penetration produced by these weapons is represented in the final couplet, whose causal relationship with the preceding quatrains is stressed by the initial *car*. The choice of the verb *navrer* (which had its full etymological force in the sixteenth century), the *trop asprement,* the *longz traictz* together with the pun contained in the expression *perceanz regardz,* all serve to intensify the total victory of Délie's aggressive glance over the Lover.

So potent are the rays emitted by Délie's eyes that not only do they slay the Lover but they are potentially lethal even to Délie herself. Scève presents what is the ultimate testimony to the eyes' power, for, having established Délie's superiority over gods and men alike, he makes her potentially vulnerable to one thing alone, her own glance. In this way, the glance becomes not just an emanation from her person, but something which transcends and dominates not only the Lover but Délie herself. Once again the Lady is subsumed by her *regard*.

> Je m'esjouys quand sa face se monstre,
> Dont la beaulté peult les Cieulx ruyner:
> Mais quand ton œil droit au mien se rencontre,
> Je suis contrainct de ma teste cliner:
> Et contre terre il me fault incliner,
> Comme qui veulx d'elle ayde requerir,
> Et au danger son remede acquerir,
> Ayant commune en toy compassion.
>  Car tu ferois nous deux bien tost perir.
> Moy du regard, toy par reflection. (Dizain 186)

Scève has recourse once again to the symbol of the basilisk, which had characterised Délie's glance in the opening poem of the collection. The deadly quality of the basilisk's stare is alluded to in the last two lines but it is implicit throughout since the basilisk appears in the emblem which immediately precedes this poem. The engraving represents a basilisk looking at itself in a mirror and has as its motto: "Mon regard par toy me tue," so that the lethal aspect of Délie's gaze is paramount right from the outset. Indeed the whole dizain investigates the action of seeing and the relationships it establishes between people and things. The first act of looking concerns the Lover who perceives his Beloved's face and experiences a feeling of intense joy. However, as always, an equilibrium of positive and negative forces is established and the destructive elements of Délie's gaze appear in line two where the effect of her beauty on the heavens is described ("la beaulté peult les Cieulx ruyner"). If the Lover can enjoy contemplating Délie when she is not looking at him, his joy is not lasting, for when Délie turns her gaze upon him, he cannot sustain its force and like a "piteuse Hostie," must bow his head as a sign of her victory. He is in this way placed in the same relationship to Délie as were the heavens of line two. The communion between the sufferings endured within the microcosm of the Lover and those inflicted upon the macrocosm by Délie's glance is further elaborated as the Lover not only inclines his head but prostrates himself to the ground, hoping to find consolation there, since the earth too falls victim to the cruelty of her eyes. This sacrifice of the Lover is not simply a gesture of self-preservation but is necessary for both him and his Lady, since both would succumb to her lethal gaze otherwise, the Lover directly as Délie turned her eyes upon him, she by the reflection of her gaze in his eyes (hence the other element of the emblem, the mirror, in which the basilisk contemplates itself). Not only does this dizain provide eloquent testimony to the effects of Délie's gaze, but it demonstrates that the life and death aspects of the love experience, which hitherto have been associated only with the Lover, extend to Délie also, so that the two are joined in a cosmic intertwining of destinies. By the act of sacrifice and submission he performs in the poem, the Lover is able to preserve both himself and Délie from mutual destruction.

In Dizain 197, the theme of the superior power of Délie's glance is not utilised. Instead, we find the eyes' action on the Lover expressed in terms of a fundamental opposition:

> Doulce ennemye, en qui ma dolente ame
> Souffre trop plus, que le corps martyré,
> Ce tien doulx œil, qui jusqu'au cœur m'entame
> De ton mourant à le vif attiré
> Si vivement, que pour le coup tiré
> Mes yeulx pleurantz employent leur deffence.
>   Mais n'y povant ne force, ne presence,
> Le Cœur criant par la bouche te prie

De luy ayder a si mortelle offence.
Qui tousjours ard, tousjours a l'ayde crie.

The essence of the poem is expressed in the opening apostrophe: *Doulce ennemye,* the Petrarchan paradox not only restating the ambivalent nature of the love relationship but at the same time establishing the first opposition which in spite of its antithetical terms in fact forms a unity, a *coincidentia oppositorum.* As usual, the instrument by which the Lady inflicts suffering is her gaze and if body and soul are united in their common martyrdom, it is by the workings of "ce tien doulx œil," the adjective creating an immediate link with *doulce ennemye* and recalling implicitly the negative part of this description of the Lady. Once again, the Lover is seen as a trinity of physiological and psychological parts and not only body and soul are wounded by the penetrating gaze but the heart, which is the source of life, is also pierced. The parallelism between the *doulce ennemye* and the "ce tien doulx œil" is stressed at the end of their respective lines by the fact that "*dolente ame*" contains the verb *entame* which is the rhyme word of line three, thus anticipating the action of the eye, while at the same time underlining the community of suffering between the soul and the heart. However, the eye is not merely the instrument of suffering, it threatens the Lover with death, here not the death that follows a mortal wound, but the love-death which occurs in the Neo-Platonic traditions when the soul leaves the Lover's body to dwell in that of the Beloved. The eye not only shoots forth a wounding arrow ("le coup *tiré*") but acts as a force attracting ("at*tire*") the Lover's soul back with it to the Beloved. The action of the eye is linked to another opposition *mourant/vif,* stressed by the polyptoton *vi/vivement* which reinforces the initial paradox contained in *doulce ennemye.* The eye wounds and brings a death to the Lover which is not death, since the Lover continues to live in the Beloved. The Lover is *ton mourant* and yet *le vif* is not destroyed even at the verbal level of the poem, but lives on in the adverb *vivement.* It is in vain that the Lover attempts to resist this violation of his most essential being and the Lover's weeping eyes are no match for his Lady's eye. At the same time as the participle *pleurantz* describes the Lover's suffering, it both recalls *mourant* thanks to its participial form and also introduces the first term of yet another

opposition which will not be completed until the last line of the
poem with *pleurantz/ard*. The only recourse of the heart (which is
the source of *le vif*) is to appeal to the Beloved, and the desperate
nature of the request is accentuated by the alliteration *"cœur criant"*
and the phonetic similarity between *"cri-*ant" and "p-*rie*." The
heart's cry remains ominously unanswered and the poem concludes
with a general maxim expressing the hopelessness of the Lover's
plight, thus making him a kind of universal representative of the
sufferings of love. His passion is expressed in terms of the traditional
metaphor of fire which provides the other part of the water/fire
antithesis established in line six and restates the contradictory condition of the Lover previously expressed in the *mourant/vif* opposition. At the same time the perpetual nature of the Lover's
suffering is stressed, as is the futility of any request for help. So in
the second half of the poem's concluding maxim, the words *ayde*
and *crie* previously related to the Lover's heart are used to express
the universality of the sufferings of love.

In Dizain 197, the negative aspects of the Neo-Platonic love-
death were to the fore, with the accent on the Lover's suffering
and hopeless struggles. Later in the cycle this theme is treated
again, once more by way of eye imagery, but in a more neutral
fashion:

> Amour lustrant tes sourcilz Hebenins,
> Avecques toy contre moy se conseille:
> Et se monstrant humainement benings,
> Le moindre d'eulx mille mortz m'appareille.
>   Arcz de structure en beaulté nompareille,
> A moy jadis immortel argument,
> Vous estes seul, & premier instrument
> Qui liberté, & la raison offence.
>   Car qui par vous conclut resolument
> Vivre en aultruy, en soy mourir commence. (Dizain 270)

The eyes' role is once again paramount in the love experience, as
Délie's eyebrows are implicitly compared to Cupid's how. Here the
eyebrows are not simply the "model" of the God of Love's weapon,
but are the basis of a pact formed between Délie and Cupid against
the Lover. The eyebrows are ebony coloured as in the *Blason du
sourcil* (to which Scève makes implicit reference in line six of this
dizain) and this enables the poet to introduce a chiaroscuro effect

by his use of the verb *lustrant* (which means "to brighten," "to give light to" rather than "to look at" as McFarlane suggests in his notes on this dizain). So the eyes, through their attendant eyebrows are once again associated not only with arrows but with light, and this light is supplied by Cupid himself. The power of the eyes/ eyebrows is deadly, since the least of them — each hair forming the eyebrows being compared to an arrow — can bring not just death, but "*mille* mortz" to the Lover. Yet the effect of this hyperbole is tempered by the preceding line, as the positive aspect of the eyes' glances is evoked, for in their attack they are paradoxically "humainement benings."

In the second quatrain of the poem, the poet-lover makes reference to the *Blason du sourcil,* while at the same time describing the eyebrows with an architectural metaphor ("Arcz de structure en beauté nompareille") as in the *Blason*. The immortality this poem had brought him in the past is contrasted with the thousand deaths he is presently undergoing and the eyebrows' attack on the freedom and reason of the Lover is mentioned. The poem's final couplet links the eyebrow/Cupid/arrow imagery to the theme of the death unto self in love. That it does so with the causative connective *car* is further proof of the inevitability of this occurrence. Yet if these two lines share the maxim-like quality of Dizain 197 discussed previously, here there is the suggestion that the Lover is not the unwilling victim but a partner in the love relationship, albeit a subordinate one: "Car qui par vous *conclut resolument/* Vivre ne aultruy en soy mourir."

In Dizain 290, the eye is not simply an aggressive attacker penetrating the innermost recesses of the Lover's being, it is also an agent of transformation and we witness a veritable metamorphosis of the Lover who desires to become one with the source of both his suffering and joy.

> Comme gelée au monter du Soleil,
> Mon ame sens, qui toute se distille
> Au rencontrer le rayant de son œil,
> Dont le povoir me rend si fort debile,
> Que je devien tous les jours moins habile
> A resister aux amoureux traictz d'elle.
>     En la voyant ainsi plaisamment belle,
> Et le plaisir croissant de bien en mieulx

Par une joye incongneue, & novelle,
Que ne suis donc plus, qu'Argus, tout en yeulx?

Here the Beloved's eye is identified with the eye of the universe, the sun, as the Lover's microcosm responds to the lightbeams projected from Délie's eyes, just as the natural world reacts to the sun's rays. As Staub has noted in his excellent commentary on this dizain, "la poésie de Scève est mouvement" and the dynamics of the poet's transfiguration are linked to the over-increasing strength of Délie's glance. [16] There is a parallel but opposite movement present in the first six lines of the poem. As the sun rises in the sky and as Délie's gaze increases in intensity, the inner unity and strength of the Lover is progressively destroyed. From the hard compactness of the initial *gelée* ("frost"), he progresses to the liquidity of *se distiller,* from implicit strength he becomes both *fort debile* and *moins habile.* Yet this initial strength and unity, like the Lover's freedom before the irruption of Délie into his soul, is only apparently positive. The fact that the image chosen to represent the Lover's original oneness is also endowed with the negative sign of coldness, demonstrates that this is scarcely a desirable state and will not resist the positive sign of heat which is an integral part of Délie's gaze. The progressive weakening of resistance, the melting of the Lover's hard, icy soul and its vulnerability to the *amoureux traictz* launched from Délie's eyes, are, as Staub has pointed out: "la condition nécessaire pour que la force bienfaisante de Délie puisse la (l'âme) pénétrer et la faire revivre." [17]

The transformation from hard to soft, from cold to hot becomes entirely positive in the last four lines of the poem. All negative and ambiguous elements are banished as the Lover basks in the flames of love projected by Délie's eyes. Délie is *plaisamment belle* and the pleasure derived from contemplating her beauty is transferred to the Lover in the following line as the noun *plaisir* becomes descriptive of his state of mind. This pleasure is not, however, static, but dynamic as it increases from *bien* to *mieulx,* bringing a new, unknown joy of infinite dimensions. As before, love brings knowledge, expanding the Lover's spiritual and emotional horizons to

---

[16] Staub, op. cit., p. 35.
[17] Ibid.

encompass the previously unknown and unexperienced. This expansion parallels the desire for transformation, as the Lover expresses the wish to become another Argus, to be metamorphosed into the organ of sight, which is also the principal means by which knowledge about both the physical and ideal world is obtained. In this way, he will be totally receptive to the beneficial effects of her love, transmitted by her gaze which penetrates his soul through the gateway of his own eyes. This desire also represents his wish for total identification with the source of love who is here, as elsewhere, pure gaze. Scève's wish here anticipates M. de Wolmar: "Si je pouvais changer la nature de mon être et devenir un œil vivant je ferais volontiers cet échange." [18]

The salutory effects of the suffering inflicted by Délie's wounding glance is the subject of Dizain 390, but here the onslaught of her eyes first provokes a movement of retreat rather than attraction on the part of the Lover's soul:

> Toutes les fois que je voy eslever
> Tes haultz sourcilz, & leurs cornes ployer
> Pour me vouloir mortellement grever,
> Ou tes durz traictz dessus moy employer,
> L'Ame craignant si dangereux loyer,
> Se pert en moy, comme toute paoureuse.
> O si tu es de mon vivre amoureuse,
> De si doulx arcz ne crains la fureur telle.
> Car eulx cuidantz donner mort doloureuse,
> Me donnent vie heureuse, & immortelle.

Scève returns to one of his favourite metonymies for the eyes, the eyebrows, which because of their shape are compared to horns and are therefore implicitly associated with the crescent moon, another symbol for Délie's power of cruelty which had already been used in Dizain 106 ("Car lors jectant ses cornes la Deesse . . ."). Once more there is a parallel movement at work in the first part of this dizain: a movement of elevation on the part of the eyebrows which produces a contrary movement of descent by the Lover's soul. Like the rising new moon, Délie's eyebrows ascend, but they do so in order to plunge their wounding hornlike points into the Lover's

---

[18] Jean-Jacques Rousseau, *La Nouvelle Héloïse* (Paris: Garnier, 1960), p. 474.

soul. The *moy* of the poem is overshadowed and threatened by the *durs traictz* associated with Délie's eyes and brows, and the soul retreats downwards into the Lover's body, overcome with fear at the suffering augured by the Lady's fearsome weapons. However, the sufferings of love are fruitful and in an apostrophe to his soul, the Lover begs it not to fear the eyes' menace. Suddenly the intimidating weapons change their aspect. Not only do they become *doulx arcz,* thus acquiring the favourable epithet Scève uses to describe the beneficial characteristics of love, but they also become essential to the Lover's very existence ("[...] si tu es de mon vivre amoureuse") and produce the opposite effect from that expected by the cowering soul. Instead of the expected *mort douloureuse,* they bring *vie heureuse* and this transformation is skilfully underlined by the use of the expressions *donner mort* and *donnent vie,* the change in grammatical form from infinitive to active verb being further highlighted by the antithetical pair *douloureuse/heureuse,* which are linked by a very effective interior rhyme. In the same way *mort* is transformed by polyptoton into its opposite *immortelle,* so that once more we have a complete metamorphosis of the situation presented at the beginning of the dizain, a metamorphosis which hinges on the ambivalent and paradoxical might of the Beloved's gaze.

The physical and spiritual aspects of the love experience also come into play in Dizain 424, which recounts the effects of Délie's beauty and perfection upon both the outer and inner worlds. Here the workings of the eye are fundamental not only to the thematics of the poem but occupy lines five to seven: the geographical centre of the dizain:

> De corps tresbelle & d'ame bellissime,
> Comme plaisir, & gloire a l'Univers,
> Et en vertu rarement rarissime
> Engendre en moy mille souciz divers:
> Mesmes son œil pudiquement pervers
> Me penetrant le vif du sentement,
> Me ravit tout en tel contentement.
> Que du desir est ma joye remplie,
> La voyant l'œil, aussi l'entendement,
> Parfaicte au corps, & en l'ame accomplie.

The essence of the description of Délie's beauty is unity and harmony. Here body and soul are not antithetical but complementary, a fact stressed by the use of parallel syntax in the first line (*de/* noun/adjective) and of the same adjectival nucleus *belle* which is *tresbelle* for *corps* and *bellissime* for *l'ame,* the superlative form underlining the superiority of the spiritual over the corporal despite their fusion. The initial pair *corps/ame* generates another duo of laudatory terms in line two, *plaisir/gloire,* the former being associated by its position in the poetic line with corporal pleasure, *gloire* with the spiritual. Yet both form a unity which is attached to *l'Univers,* showing that perfect beauty is both a physical and spiritual union and that both are necessary to bring pleasure and glory to the Universe.

The final element in this encomium of Délie is the excellence of her *vertu,* an essentially spiritual quality. However, the noun is accompanied by two dependent words constructed on the same stem: *rarement* and *rarissime.* This technique, by recalling the *tresbelle/bellissime* couple of line one and its association with *corps* and *ame* suggests that both body and soul are important in producing *vertu rarement rarissime.* Up to this point in the poem, the description of Délie's beauty and virtue has been static, plastic and monumental. Her effect on the macrocosm is described by the use of simple prepositions without the help of any verb. However, the Lover lives in a world of flux and when Délie works her magic on his microcosm, we again find ourselves in the presence of the dynamic movement so often associated with the workings of love. The first verb of the poem, *engendre,* acts upon the *moy* of the Lover and describes the inner turmoil which the sight of Délie's beauty provokes within him. Once again her eye is the central agent of aggression and the ambivalence of its penetration is expressed through the antithetical *pudiquement pervers.* However, in spite of the disturbing elements of Love's aggression and its penetration to *le vif du sentement,* the cares of love (*mille souciz divers*) do yield to contentment and joy. The dual nature of Délie's beauty, physical and spiritual, is again underlined by the pairing of words: *pudiquement pervers* whose alliteration in "p" suggests the basic synthesis of apparently antithetical elements, and *sentement* and *contentement,* whose relationship is stressed by their common formation and by their rich rhyme. The words *desir* and *joie* also evoke the twofold nature of the love which Délie begets, and in the last two lines of the poem, the word *l'œil* — here the Lover's eye which receives the penetrating beams from Délie's eyes — represents above all the perception of physical beauty, while it is the inner eye of *l'entendement,* which apprehends the spiritual perfection of the Lady. In the final line, harmony and order are imposed upon the Lover's soul and the same kind of tranquility which characterised the reaction of Nature to Délie's beauty in the early part of the dizain, descends upon him, as he recognises the perfect union of her physical and spiritual perfection. The repetition of the words *corps* and *ame* and the balanced structure of the last line recall the opening line of the dizain so that we have a circular movement, revolving around the emanations from Délie's eyes to the eye of the Lover, a circularity which also suggests the shape of the organ of sight, engendering on her part, receiving on his, the beams of Love.

## 2)  *The Eye as Source of Venom*

Closely allied to the representation of the eyes as wounding, piercing weapons is their depiction as emitters of poison which carry the infection of love to the eye receiving their emanations. As we have already seen, this is a common feature of the aggressive eye topos and is found in authors from Classical Antiquity to the time of the Renaissance. Although the first dizain of the *Délie* presents the Lady's eyes as a sharp knife, lance or arrow, the theme of the poisonous eye is implicit in the image of the basilisk which was held to be a member of the serpent family. This aspect of the initial dizain's imagery is developped in Dizain three of the work. The preceding dizain concerns Délie's perfection and this poem's sphere of action is the heavens ("Le Naturant par ses haultes Idées [. . .]"). However, if for the rest of mankind, Délie is associated with the celestial and with joy and pleasure ("[. . .] de tous la delectation"), the last line of the second dizain marks a sharp movement of descent and of antithesis with the rest of the poem, since for the Lover, at least at this point in his itinerary, Délie is associated with the infernal: "[. . .] de moy seul fatale Pandora." The downward movement is continued in Dizain 3:

> Ton doulx venin, grace tienne, me fit
> Idolatrer en ta divine image

Dont l'œil credule ignoramment meffit
Pour non preveoir a mon futur dommage.
   Car te immolant ce mien cœur pour hommage
Sacrifia avec l'Ame la vie.
   Doncques tu fus, ô liberté ravie,
Donnée en proye a toute ingratitude:
Doncques espere avec deceue envie
Aux bas Enfers trouver beatitude.

While Délie's eyes are not explicitly mentioned as the source of
the *doulx venin,* the connection is obvious, given both the elements
of the aggressive eye topos and the context of this poem within the
*Délie.* The emanations from the Lady's eyes are once again endowed
with ambiguous positive-negative signs, which ever since the *paour
d'agreables terreurs* of Dizain 1, characterise Scevian love. The poem
is constructed around another set of opposites, the divine of *ta
divine image* which the sweet love-poison forces the Lover to worship, and the infernal, which appears explicitly at the end of the
dizain and towards which the whole movement of the poem is
directed. The Lover's worship depends not only on Délie's gaze
which transmits her poison, but on his own receptive eyes which
allow the poison to gain entrance into his soul. What the Lover
idolatrises is the Lady's *divine image, image* having both the sense
of "likeness" but also carrying its full association with the act of
seeing. It is the Lover's own eyes that betray him here ("l'œil
credule ignoramment meffit") and are represented as the cause of
his *futur dommage.* The worship of an idol involves human sacrifice
and as the word *venin* already suggested, death is to be the outcome
of this fatal meeting of eyes. It is the Lover's eye which performs
the offering, as it immolates his heart, the source of his life, to the
Beloved, at the same time yielding both his soul and his very life
to Délie. Death is the natural result in view of the ingratitude
manifested by Délie. The only hope for the Lover is an apparently
vain one: that of finding *beatitude* (normally associated with the
heavens) "aux bas Enfers," the site of suffering and death. The
descending movement is completed. The Lover after his self-im-
molation on the altar of love for Délie, is lingering in Hades and
yet he is not without hope, for despite her ingratitude, Délie is also
associated with the infernal regions through Hecate and so is, po-

tentially at least, present even in the depths where the Lover finds
himself.

In Dizain 42, the *doulx venin* is explicitly associated with Délie's
eyes and a semi-physiological description of the progressive possession of the body by the poison follows:

> Si doulcement le venin de tes yeulx
> Par mesme lieu aux fonz du cœur entra,
> Que sans douleur le desir soucyeux
> De liberté tout seul il rencontra.
> Mais l'occupant, peu a peu, penetra,
> Ou l'Ame libre en grand seurté vivoit:
>   Alors le sang, qui d'elle charge avoit,
> Les membres laisse & fuit au profond Puys
> Voulant cacher le feu, que chascun voit.
> Lequel je couvre, & celer ne le puis.

This is the first dizain of the fifth group of nine and is preceded
by an emblem depicting an unadorned lantern with the motto
"Celer ne le puis," incorporated into the last line of the poem. As
the iconography's relationship with the thematics of the poem is
limited to the last two lines and is quite straightforward (or appears
to be), no further attention need be paid to the emblem itself in
the context of eye imagery, except the fact that the lantern, like the
eye itself, is a source of light. In this poem the *doulx* which was
attached to *venin* in Dizain 3 is present in adverbial form (*doulcement*), thus relating it grammatically to the verb *entra* and stressing
the movement of the poison through the Lover's body. The source
of the venom is explicitly mentioned here: it is "le venin de tes
yeulx" and it penetrates the Lover's body "par mesme lieu," that
is, through the eyes, so that once again the relationship transmitter/
receiver is established between Délie's eyes and the Lover's. The
venom proceeds to the depths of the heart where it encounters "le
desir soucyeux de liberté." However, so gently does the insidious
poison work its way through the body that the meeting is *sans
douleur*. The slow but sure conquest continues and the venom
gradually reaches the seat of the soul. The body's counterattack,
which takes the form of flight, comes too late and does nothing
but continue the inward trajectory of the poison. In a movement
of escape, the blood retreats to the deep well, which McFarlane
in his notes identifies as the liver, an organ considered by Renais-

sance physiology to be the seat of desire. [19] The blood by its retreat
hopes at least to conceal the fires of concupiscence which are apparent to everyone. The Lover's dilemma is complete in the closing
line of the poem. Just as the blood is unable to hide the fire of
love, so the Lover's attempt to cover and conceal his passion is to
no avail, for like the lantern in the emblem, it is visible to all. The
uselessness of the Lover's struggles is effectively brought into relief
by the rhyme *puys/puis,* the verb of endeavour being phonetically
identical with the place of concealment and negated by the accom-
panying *ne.*

Dizain 372 presents another example of the *coincidentia oppositorum* of Love, for here Délie is not only the source of love, but a
remedy against its deadly poison. This paradox is not only a poetic
transposition of the theme of the bitter-sweet nature of love, but
the association of venom with the serpent, already a phallic animal
long before Freud and associated with sin and hell from the time
of Genesis, also suggests the struggle between carnal and spiritual
love. [20] Although the love Scève describes is ideally a harmony of
the two, in many dizains [21] it is the Platonic black horse [22] which
appears to be in danger of gaining the upper hand. If the suffering
the Lover endures is due in part to the loss of his freedom and
selfhood as his soul goes to take up its abode in the Beloved, the
pangs of love come partly from the sensual desires of the Lover
who is not always indifferent to the *bien* that lovers can enjoy, a
*bien* that has very little in common with the *bien* of Platonic love. [23]

---

[19] See Jacques Ferrand, *De la maladie d'Amour* (Paris, 1623), p. 54:
"L'amour ayant abusé les yeux, comme vrays espions et portiers de l'ame, se
laisse tout doucement glisser par des canaux et cheminant insensiblement par
les veines jusques au foye, imprime soudain un desir ardent de la chose qui
est reellement, ou paroist aimable, allume la concupiscence, et par ce desir
commence toute la seduction."

[20] In his commentary on Dizain 372, Boutang has said: "Dès l'origine, la
*Délie* se manifeste comme le heurt et l'équilibre de deux thèmes: celui du
choc amoureux qui pénètre l'âme et attaque la liberté intime et celui de la
perfection de l'aimée qui transforme l'âme et la guide vers sa vérité. Les deux
amours du *Banquet* sont unis en un seul, tyrannique et contradictoire." Pierre
Boutang, *Commentaire sur 49 dizains de la Délie* (Paris, 1953), p. 125.

[21] See for example Dizain 161, the famous jealousy dizain.

[22] See Plato's *Phaedrus* where the myth of the soul as a chariot drawn
by two horses is expounded.

[23] See for example the strongly sensual Dizain 41 where the word *bien*
refers to sensual enjoyment and not to spiritual enlightenment.

Tu m'es le Cedre encontre le venin
De ce Serpent en moy continuel,
Comme ton œil cruellement benin
Me vivifie au feu perpetuel,
Alors qu'Amour par affect mutuel
T'ouvre la bouche, & en tire a voix plaine
Celle douleur celestement humaine,
Qui m'est souvent peu moins, que rigoureuse,
Dont spire (ô Dieux) trop plus suave alaine,
Que n'est Zephire en l'Arabie heureuse.

In Dizain 372 Délie is both the serpent, because she is a physical presence whose corporal beauty awakens the sensual desire of the Lover, and the antidote against this venom, the aspiration to conquer purely physical attraction and transform it into spiritual love. The cedar is chosen because it was believed that its odour chased away serpents. As Saulnier has suggested,[24] it was also thought that the cedar was harmful to man, so that even the antidote involves suffering and the symbol of Délie's curative powers contains within itself a hint of ambiguity. This ambiguity is central to the poem, for even the serpent has positive symbolic associations. If in the Judeo-Christian tradition it is allied with evil and if in the fertility rites of primitive man it was above all a phallic symbol, it is in fact polysemic and can also represent wisdom, learning and even healing, as the serpent's association with Asclepius shows. The area of ambivalence which surrounds both the predominantly positive symbol of the cedar and the predominantly negative serpent (linked however by the alliteration of their initial letters and by their placement at the caesura) becomes explicit in lines three and four. Here, Délie's eye is *cruellement benin,* a source of poison and its cure. It is also the origin of the fire which vivifies the Lover *au feu perpetuel* (which corresponds to the *en moy continuel* of line two), a fire which is the fire of love and at the same time the purifying fire of purgatorial suffering. However, while fire imagery plays an important role here, it is the cedar which directs the movement of the dizain towards the final resolution. Since it is the smell of the cedar which repels serpents and since the cedar is associated with the exotic East, the poem turns finally towards the sweet-smelling perfumes of Araby. However, before closing the dizain on this positive

---

[24] V.-L. Saulnier, *Maurice Scève* (Paris, 1948-49), I, p. 282.

note, the poet develops the paradoxical effects Délie exercises on
the Lover as she opens her mouth to speak and there issues forth
a *douleur celestement humaine,* a *douleur* which suggests the pain
which comes from the mouth of the serpent when it strikes its
victim. However, the venom of Délie's rigorous words is covered
by the sweet perfume which emanates from her mouth as she
speaks, just as the perfume of the cedar counteracted the serpent's
poison in line two. Once more it is Délie's gaze which is at the
centre of this process of transformation and which is the source
not only of the initial deadly venom, but also of the new life which
follows the irruption of love into the unsuspecting and unwilling
soul.

Dizain 388 also presents love as a poison projected from Délie's
eyes. Whereas earlier in the work its primary effects were associated with April, Spring and youth, the poet here places the love
he so minutely analyses, in the context of autumnal maturity:

> Ce doulx venin, qui de tes yeulx distille,
> M'amollit plus en ma virilité,
> Que ne feit onc au Printemps inutile
> Ce jeune Archier guidé d'agilité.
>   Donc ce Thuscan pour vaine utilité
> Trouve le goust de son Laurier amer:
> Car de jeunesse il aprint a l'aymer.
>   Et en Automne Amour, ce Dieu volage,
> Quand me voulois de la raison armer,
> A prevalu contre sens, & contre aage.

The fact that the Lover is depicted as being "en (sa) virilité," that
is, as mature and seasoned, [25] attests to the extraordinary power of
the love venom. Once more it is characterised as *doulx venin* and
it is directly attributed to the eyes of the Lady. It is more potent
than Cupid's arrows which attacked him in his youth, represented
as his *Printemps inutile (inutile,* because his youthful loves were
*jeunes erreurs* and did not have the immutability and redemptive
effects of Délie's love). There follows a rather strained comparison
with Petrarch, the sole base of which is that he began to love in

---

[25] Autumn, in the Renaissance, was generally considered to be the period
of fullest maturity, as the culmination of summer rather than the precursor
of winter.

his youth (a detail which establishes a connection with *printemps*), whereas in later life he found the taste of his *Laurier* bitter (an implied contrast with the *doulx venin* of line one). The poem returns to its principal theme in the last three lines with the attack by Cupid on the Lover's mature *sens,* the implication being that its success is due only to the alliance of Cupid with Délie and to his use of the power of her eyes.

### 3) *The Eye as Source of Fire*

In the *Délie,* the eye is sometimes represented not only as an arrow-shooter or dispenser of poison, but as a fire which projects its flames into the Lover's soul through his eyes. This depiction of the eyes' working corresponds to the "scientific" explanation of vision as found in Plato, whereby the eyes has its own illumination in the form of fire (see Chapter 1). It also brings into play the traditional association of fire with love, but combines it with the aggressive eye topos to stress the eyes' role as instigator and assailant in the love experience.

This aspect of Scève's eye imagery is illustrated in the first section of Dizain 115:

> Par ton regard severement piteux
> Tu m'esblouis premierement la veue:
> Puis du regard de son feu despiteux
> Surpris le Cœur, & l'ame a l'impourveue,
> Tant que despuis, apres mainte reveue,
> J'ars de plus fort sans novelle achoison.

We have here another of those reworkings of the *innamoramento* which are scattered throughout the *Délie* as a kind of focal point to permit us to review the initial shock of love and to see the evolution of the Lover's passion with respect to this central and fundamental event. Here the word *œil* is not used as in Dizains 1 and 6, instead the emphasis is placed on the *act* of seeing (rather than on the organ of vision) by the use of *regard*. Once more the action is described in antithetical terms by the use of the word-pair *severement piteux,* severity and pity usually being found at opposite ends of the emotional spectrum. However, the *severement* also underlines Délie's dignity and superiority, which is part of her pity for the Lover. In addition, there is a possible play on the word

*severement,* since the latinised form of the poet's name is *saevus,* a
pun which is found in two places in Pernette Du Guillet's *Rymes.* [26]
Although we have thus far scrupulously distinguished the *je poétique* of the *Délie* from the *je autobiographique* with which it is
so often identified, we have already seen one poem where the fictional Lover represented by the *je* appropriates at least one feature
of the poet's own biography (Dizain 270 where the poem's speaker
makes specific reference to the celebrity gained through the poem
*Blason du sourcil*). The fact that these occasional references do exist
in the *Délie* make a play on the word *severement* quite plausible
and even appropriate, since the object of Délie's pity is the fictional Lover of the series whom the poet makes his persona.

The effect of Délie's projected gaze is first described in terms
of light as the outer bastions of the Lover's defenses, his eyes, fall
before the onslaught. After this conquest, the trajectory of Délie's
*regard* continues, as in Dizain 1, to take by surprise the heart and
soul (*à l'impourveue* is a direct quotation from Dizain 1). Here the
Lover's innermost being is attacked not by light, but by fire projected from Délie's eyes, which, *apres mainte reveue,* have per-
petuated the inner fire of love so that it now burns ever more
strongly without any further intervention on the part of the Lady.

Dizain 207 anticipates the imagery of Dizain 290 (which we
have already discussed in the first section of this chapter), without
however using the arrow terminology which is central to the latter
poem:

> Je m'asseurois, non tant de liberté
> Heureuse d'estre en si hault lieu captive,
> Comme tousjours me tenoit en seurté
> Mon gelé cœur, donc mon penser derive,
> Et si tresfroit, qu'il n'est flambe si vive,
> Qu'en bref n'estaigne, et que tost il n'efface.
>     Mais les deux feuz de ta celeste face,
> Soit pour mon mal, ou certes pour mon heur,
> De peu a peu me fondirent ma glance,
> La distillant en amoureuse humeur.

Here we have, as in the later dizain, a metamorphosis described in
terms of heat and cold. The Lover moves from a state of certainty

---

[26] Pernette Du Guillet, *Rymes,* ed. V. Graham (Geneva, 1968): "Puis que,
de nom et de faict, trop severe / En mon endroict . . . ," Chanson VI, p. 54.

and stability, which is a false one since it is based on his mistaken self-confidence in the power of his heart to extinguish or reject the flames of love. The negative and unyielding nature of this stance is suggested by the image of the frozen heart (just as the soul is compared to *gelée* in Dizain 290), which is an unnatural state for the heart, particularly according to Renaissance physiology since it is both the seat of the emotions and the producer of the warm humour, blood. The solidity which the Lover mistakenly attributes to his heart is in fact a deathlike immobility. However, this state changes when a new, irresistible fire appears, its entrance marked by the *Mais* of line seven. This fire is identified with Délie's eyes as their flames melt the ice of the poet's heart, transforming it into the liquid of love. It is interesting that the word chosen by Scève should be *humeur,* for while its first meaning is "liquid" (from the Latin *humor*), it also evokes the four humous of Renaissance medicine, in particular the blood, since the heart was central to the first six lines. The implication is that the Lover receives not only the fires of passion from Délie's eyes but also new life, as the heart resumes its normal operation thanks to the regenerating power of her gaze.

The painful and yet beneficial effects of the flames generated by Délie's eyes are also the subject of Dizain 292:

> De ton sainct œil, Fusil sourd de ma flamme,
> Naist le grand feu, qui en mon cœur se cele:
> Aussi par l'œil il y entre, & l'enflamme
> Avecques morte, & couverte estincelle,
> Me consumant, non les flancs, non l'esselle,
> Mais celle part, qu'on doibt plus estimer,
> Et qui me fait, maulgré moy, tant aymer,
> Qu'en moy je dy telle ardeur estre doulce,
> Pour non (en vain) l'occasion blasmer
> Du mal, qui tout a si hault bien me poulse.

While the eye here is represented as flint rather than as flame, the relationship between the two is undeniable. The fire burning in the Lover's soul comes directly from the spark emanating from Délie's *sainct œil*. This spark enters through the Lover's eye and makes its way throughout the body, not attacking its outer parts but concentrating itself on the soul ("celle part, qu'on doibt (le) plus estimer"). The Lover's resistance to this all-consuming flame is evident in both the causative *me fait . . . aymer* and in the *maul-gré moy,* and yet in spite of the suffering, the effects of the fire are ultimately beneficial. The *ardeur* is therefore qualified by the adjective *doulce* and the pain is an instigation to uplifting and puri-fication. So the downward movement begun in the opening section of the dizain, as the eye's flames, placed in the highest realm by its adjective *sainct,* descend into the depths of the Lover's soul, is transformed into a movement of elevation as the soul seeks the *si hault bien* inspired in him by the conflagration of Délie's love in his soul.

## 4) *The Eye as Lightning*

Closely related to the representation of the Beloved's eyes as a source of fire and incorporating the same type of aggressivity as the weapon imagery so often associated with the organ of sight is their depiction as lightning flashes.[27] Whereas images of fire stress both the warmth and pain of love, lightning becomes a symbol of the suddenness and the capriciousness of the bolt of love, while at the same time containing connotations of bedazzlement and pain. Lightning also associates Délie's eyes with the heavens and with the omnipotence of Jupiter.

The first dizain in the work where the eyes' workings are ex-plicitly compared with the action of lightning is Dizain 24, the first dizain of the third group of nine, preceded by Emblem III.

> Quand l'œil aux champs est d'esclairs esblouy,
> Luy semble nuict quelque part, qu'il regarde:
> Puis peu a peu de clarté resjouy,
> Des soubdains feuz du Ciel se contregarde.
> 　Mais moy conduict dessoubs la sauvegarde
> De ceste tienne, & unique lumiere,
> Qui m'offusca ma lyesse premiere
> Par tes doulx rayz aiguement suyviz,
> Ne me pers plus en veue coustumiere.
> 　Car seulement pour t'adorer je vis.

---

[27] Gilbert Durand has suggested a direct connection between the arrow (which as we have seen is the most frequent weapon associated with the eye) and the lightning flash. See *Les Structures anthropologiques de l'imaginaire* (Paris, 1963), p. 137: "La flèche (. . .) serait symbole du savoir rapide et son doublet est alors le rayon instantanée qu'est l'éclair."

The emblem, as McFarlane describes it, [28] represents "a man holding a stick, on a pedestal, contemplating a large lamp." The lamp, which is also presumably the idol mentioned in the title of the emblem ("La lampe et l'idole"), occupies the centre of the losange and recalls the closing lines of the first dizain: "Piteuse hostie au conspect de toy, Dame, / Constituée Idole de ma vie." The lamp appears to have two flames, which would then be symbolic of Délie's eyes and the man with the stick is reminiscent of the pilgrim whose journey is entirely centred upon a single object of worship. "The pedestal," as McFarlane calls it, is certainly a raised platform of some sort, although it is dominated by the lamp which is even higher, but it could equally well be an altar, which would be perhaps more in keeping with the basic symbolism of the *Délie*. The motto, "pour te adorer je vis," is the last line of the dizain with the addition of the causal *car* and the adverb *seulement.*

The dizain itself is divided into three parts, an initial quatrain, a group of five lines and a single concluding line bearing the emblem's motto. The eye, which figures so prominently in the first line, is the same singular passive receptor as in Dizains 1 and 6, and as in those two previous poems, it is attacked and overcome by a superior, external force. This victory is represented in terms of darkness and light, for the excess of light dispensed by the lightning dazzles the Lover's eye (the close relationship between the lightning and its effect being stressed by their proximity in the line and by their common initial vowel, so that the blinding light of line one brings the *nuict* of line two). Coupled with this antithesis is the implicit contrast between the word *champs,* representing the earth, and the *esclairs* which came from the heavens, a contrast made explicit in line four when the *du Ciel* corresponds in the antithetical mode to the *aux champs* of line one. However, despite the obvious conection between the *œil* of the first quatrain and the Lover, this quatrain describes a natural phenomenon and in nature, the eye, which is blinded by lightning, gradually regains its sight (the *clarté* of line three) and takes precautions to safeguard itself against future harm.

The *Mais moy* of the poem's second section indicates immediately that the situation of the Lover, while in some ways similar

[28] McFarlane, op. cit., p. 132.

to that of the *œil* of line one, is at the same time significantly different. While the Lover was blinded by the lightning-like rays from Délie's eyes (which are nevertheless *doulx*) and experienced the same darkness as the eye of line one (*offusca* comes from the Latin *offuscare,* to darken), his constant exposure to this source of light is his protection, so that while the natural eye "des soubdains feuz du Ciel se contregarde," the Lover's vulnerable eye is now "dessoubs la sauvegarde / De ceste tienne, & unique lumiere," which leads to the state described in line nine, a static pose (like that of the emblem's figure) of rest and safety. Although this line is quite obscure, the several possible readings all point to the positiveness of the Lover's situation. [29] This movement towards final stability is affirmed in the last line of the poem which contains the emblem's motto linked to the preceding lines by *car* and strengthened by *seulement.* The overwhelming importance of the eye in this love transaction is recapitulated in the final verb *je vis,* which while it is here the present tense of *vivre* also evokes the past definite of *voir,* so that life and sight are again implicitly linked.

Dizain 80 uses much of the terminology of Dizain 24 to recapitulate the *innamoramento*:

> Au recevoir l'aigu de tes esclairs
> Tu m'offuscas & sens, & congnoissance.
> Car par leurs rays si soubdains, & si clairs,
> J'eu premier peur, & puis resjouissance:
> Peur de tumber soubz griefve obeissance:
> Joye de veoir si hault bien allumer.
>    Osas tu donc de toy tant presumer,
> Œil esblouy, de non veoir, & de croire,
> Qu'en me voulant a elle accoustumer,
> Facilement j'obtiendrois la victoire?

---

[29] McFarlane suggests that "en veue coustumiere" means "having got used to beholding," in which case the line would mean something like: "having got used to beholding her (and therefore no longer being dazzled by her light), I no longer become lost (as I used to) in the darkness which follows the initial *éblouissement*." However, the expression could also mean "habitual mode of seeing," which would indicate either that he has not recovered his normal sight but that in any case this has no importance since his present state is better that his usual mode of seeing; or that he no longer loses himself in the vain pastime of looking at other objects but would rather contemplate only Délie. This reading would appear to be more appropriate in view of the *car* of the last line.

The initial shock comes from the Beloved's eyes and has its effect through the medium of the Lover's sight. As in Dizain 1, the penetrating quality of Délie's gaze is stressed, here by the adjectival noun *l'aigu* which, when applied to the image of *tes esclairs,* transforms the lightning flashes from Délie's eyes into an atmospheric variant of *sa poignant' veue.* Once again the result of so much light is its antithesis, darkness, and the verb *offuscas* is used to show the effect both on the senses and on the spirit of the Lover. Not only is his physical sight dazzled by the radiant beauty of Délie, but his consciousness suffers the same fate. And yet the darkness which follows the flash of light is only partially negative. The sudden bright lightning flashes bring firstly fear, but then joy (*resjouissance*). In fact the fear/joy couple is but one of a number of similar pairs which form the basic structure of the first six lines of this dizain. The two most important pairs are *peur/resjouissance* and *sens/congnoissance* which stand in parallel if opposite relationship to each other. The fear which is the Lover's first emotion when struck by the Beloved's gaze is related to his senses or to the lower part of the love experience. The fear is explained in line five as the fear of falling *soubz griefve obeissance,* of losing personal independence and freedom, of having to submit to the Other. The fear is akin to the struggles of the old sensual man mentioned by Saint Paul. *Congnoissance* is also a function of the eye, as we learned from Plato, and the Lover's eye not only receives the image of physical beauty but with it the deeper and higher knowledge which is the true purpose of love and desire. Thus the *congnoissance* which is affected after the *sens,* leads to *resjouissance* explained in line six as the joy at seeing "si hault bien allumer." Having made the connection between these two semantic units we can form a paradigm within the first six lines which links the *aigu* of the phrase "l'aigu de tes esclairs" to *sens* and to *peur,* representing the painful tortures of sensual love and the unwillingness to replace the selfishness of this type of love by the altruism of a more spiritual love. Similarly, *esclairs,* a heavenly phenomenon, forms a secondary unit with *congnoissance* and *resjouissance,* just as *soubdains* in line three, belongs to the negative *aigu/peur* side of the ledger, while *clairs* can be placed in the positive *congnoissance* column. The ambivalent character we constantly find attributed to the love experience in the *Délie* is a complex phenomenon, but it is clear from this ex-

ample that at least one dimension of the problem is to be found
in the struggle between sensual love, equated with death and with
self-centredness, and spiritual love, equated with a submission
which, while painful, brings new life through the virtue and grace
of the Lady. That Scève's Lover only manages to resolve the conflict between the two at the very end of the work is made evident
by the fact that the ambivalent nature of love is still part of the
thematics of Dizains 447 and 448. It is only in the final dizain
that harmony and equilibrium finally obtain.

We find the lightning imagery figuring prominently in Dizain
212, which also recalls the *innamoramento* but makes of it, not a
beginning of love situated in the past, but a continuous experience,
constantly present in the Lover's soul:

> Tes beaulx yeulx clers fouldroyamment luisantz
> Furent object a mes pensers unique,
> Des que leurs rayz si doulcement nuisantz
> Furent le mal tressainctement inique.
> Duquel le coup penetrant tousjours picque
> Croissant la playe oultre plus la moytié.
>    Et eulx estantz doulx venin d'amytié,
> Qui se nourrit de pleurs, plainctz, & lamentz,
> N'ont peu donner par honneste pitié
> Un tant soit peu de trefve a mes tourmentz.

Here, the linguistic vehicle of the lightning metaphor is, unusually,
the adverb *fouldroyamment* which modifies the adjectives of light
which describe the *yeulx* of line one. Although the initial shock
apparently leads here above all to a spiritual, rather than to a physical falling-in-love, since the eyes become the *unique object* of the
Lover's thoughts, the ambivalence of the love state is constantly
stressed throughout the dizain and the total impression is not one
of ultimate joy, as in Dizain 80, but rather of persistent suffering.
The rays from Délie's eyes are *doulcement nuisantz* (a mixture of
positive and negative), they are (or cause) "le mal tressainctement
inique" (negative/positive/negative). The initial blow is not only
still operative in the sense that its pain is still present, but it is
actively working to increase the size of the wound inflicted.

The closing quatrain brings no relief, for the poison image is
introduced into the poem, and while it is softened by the addition
of two positive words, *doulx* and *amytié,* it results in three neg-

atives: "pleurs, plainctz & lamentz," so that no consolation is obtained from the Lady's *honneste pitié* and the final word of the
dizain, *tourmentz,* sums up the whole mood of the poem. Although
certain of the elements of this piece do suggest sensual love ("le
coup penetrant," "picque" and the "venin" which evokes the phallic
serpent), it is not at all certain that this is the sole cause of the
Lover's torment. Here it is as though the harmful effects of the Beloved's glance are inseparable from the love experience and that
without suffering, which is not always the result of the Lover's
evil or sensual desires, no purification and no progress are possible,
since not even the *honneste pitié* of the Beloved's look is of any
help. It appears that her glance is after all most effective when
she remains aloof, cruel and distant, and that the more human she
becomes, the less she is able to act as a semi-divine Idol and Guide
to the tormented Lover.

## 5) *The Eye as Source of Blinding Light*

Closely related to the imagery which compares the emanations
from the Beloved's eyes to lightning, are those manifestations of
the aggressive eye topos where the eye is more generally seen as
a dispenser of light, as Sun or as another light-emitting heavenly
body. Of course, images of light (and darkness) are frequent in the
*Délie* and it is certainly not unusual to find images of light applied
to the organ of vision, the eye. The type of imagery we will examine
in this section is, however, only that which is related to the aggression and dominion of the Beloved's eyes over the Lover, and in
this respect, the light imagery which concerns us is often a variant
of the most fundamental expression of the eye's power, that of a
sharp and lethal weapon. At other times, it is less explicitly associated with the initial moment of penetration and dazzling, but
always has the element of superiority and aggressive influence over
the Lover's life and destiny.

In the first six lines of Dizain 12 we find the first representation in the *Délie* of the eyes' action expressed in terms of light:

> Ce lyen d'or, raiz de toy mon Soleil,
> Qui par le bras t'asservit Ame, & vie,
> Detient si fort avec la veue l'œil,
> Que ma pensée il t'à toute ravie,
> Me demonstrant, certes, qu'il me convie

A me stiller tout soubz ton habitude.
   Heureux service en libre servitude,
Tu m'apprens donc estre trop plus de gloire,
Souffrir pour une en sa mansuetude,
Que d'avoir eu de toute aultre victoire.

Here the image is interwoven with the traditional Petrarchan metaphor of the Beloved's hair, and yet Scève, as is almost always the case, has used the traditional material with such skill that the usual connotation of the strand of hair as a cord which binds, is enriched with a new density here thanks to its juxtaposition with light imagery. The result is that the *lyen d'or* becomes a ray of light, projected by the sun, capturing the Lover as, traditionally, hair was supposed to do. Here the Lady is identified as *mon Soleil,* and is thus placed at the centre of the Lover's own cosmos. This identification associates her with the action of her eyes, both because they are the organs which project rays of light, and because in the microcosm/macrocosm analogy, the Sun is depicted as the eye of the universe, just as the eye is the light of the body.[30] This golden ray is the instrument of conquest, which enslaved both soul and life to Délie-Sun, as the internal rhyme *asservit/vie* stresses. That the *lyen d'or* has been permanently transmuted into the realm of light and sight,[31] is quite obvious in line three where the Lover's eye is held captive *avec la veue* and the image of the Beloved has penetrated within the Lover's body so that his thoughts are completely centred upon her. The result is the modelling of the Lover in Délie's image, and here the enslavement motif is positive, as the final quatrain makes clear. It is better to be Délie's slave than any other lady's master.

The relationship between the force of Délie's gaze and the aggressive power of the Sun is developed further in Dizain 92:

---

[30] See Leone Ebreo, op. cit., p. 184: "Adunque cosí come ne l'uomo (che è piccol mondo) l'occhio, fra tutte le sue parti corporee, è come l'intelletto fra tutte le virtú de l'anima, simulacro e seguace di quella, cosé nel gran mondo il sole fra tutti i corporali à come l'intelletto divino fra tutti gli spirituali, suo simulacro e suo vero seguace."
[31] It is not uncommon to depict the sun's rays as being like strands of hair or even as a wig of light, but usually this is kept quite separate from the hair as bond motif.

Sur nostre chef gettant Phebus ses rayz,
Faisoit bouillir de son cler jour la None:
Advis me fut de veoir en son taint frais
Celle, de qui la rencontre m'estonne,
De qui la voix si fort en l'ame tonne
Que ne puis d'elle un seul doulx mot ouir:
Et de qui l'œil vient ma veue esblouir,
Tant qu'aultre n'est, fors elle, a mes yeux belle.
    Me pourra donc tel Soleil resjouir,
Quand tout Mydi m'est nuict, voire eternelle?

The natural setting which the poet depicts in the opening lines is obviously highly symbolic and gives him a poetic pretext to compare the Sun and Délie. Firstly, Phoebus (and we should remember that Délie, by her name, is associated with the moon and is hence Phoebus-Apollo's sister) is dynamically personified as casting his rays onto the heads of the lovers. The heat generated by his onslaught not only makes the day hot but suggests the fire of their passion, so that the movement from sun to Délie in line three is made almost inevitable. Délie is defined first by her likeness to the sun (and therefore as both "gettant [...] ses rays" and as causing great heat), then by her effect upon the Lover, who was thunderstruck (*estonner* is derived from *ex-tonare*) at first glimpse of her, when her eye, like that of Phoebus, dazzled him completely. Here the sun imagery produces the same result as the lightning we have previously examined: in presenting the overpowering image of Délie's beauty to the Lover's gaze, he is blinded by its radiance and so light produces its antithesis, darkness, and the sight of beauty brings suffering. This is the point of the aphoristic closing lines of the poem: can such a sun bring him joy when because of her initial effect of him he is now so blind that even mid-day seems to him like eternal night? This endless darkness evokes both the absence of the sun and also death. It refers implicitly to both the infernal side of Délie's nature, but also to the kind of death which comes to the Lover when his soul leaves him to try and seek reunion with the Beloved.

The light/darkness antithesis and its relationship to the eyes' ravishing the Lover's soul, is also the subject of Dizain 269:

Ces deux Soleilz nuisamment penetrantz,
Qui de mon vivre ont eu si long Empire,

> Par l'œil au Cœur tacitement entrantz
> Croissent le mal, qui au guerir m'empire.
>   Car leur clarté esblouissamment pire
> A son entrée en tenebres me met:
> Puis leur ardeur en joye me remet,
> M'esclairant tout au fort de leurs alarmes
> Par un espoir, qui rien mieulx ne promet,
> Qu'ardentz souspirs estainctz en chauldes larmes.

Here Délie's eyes are not suns by analogy as in Dizain 92, but by
direct metaphor, and are symbolic of the power and attraction of
the Lady. The two suns of line one suggest the lethal, weapon-like
quality of the Beloved's gaze, as its penetration operates through
the medium of the Lover's own eye and proceeds to his heart. The
result is the Lover's suffering and yet this suffering is paradoxically
presented as being beneficial, for as Délie's rays increase *le mal,*
making the Lover's condition worse, they also heal.

The paradox is elaborated in lines five and six where the light
from Délie's eyes brings darkness to the Lover. An upswing of
emotion follows as the poet turns his attention, not to the light,
but to the fire emanating from these two suns. This *ardeur* brings
joy and light even in the midst of the *alarmes* brought by the action
of her gaze; however the joy is transitory, since it is founded on
a false hope, the hope of Délie's favour. In fact, the Lover is once
again plunged into suffering in the last lines of the poem, a suffering expressed through another antithesis generated by the *ardeur*
of line seven. Here we have another example of the way in which
Scève revitalises the Petrarchan arsenal of images. The traditional
attributes of the despondent lover, "sighs and tears," are here
woven into the metaphorical framework of the dizain by the addition of two attributive adjectives and form a double paradox which
expresses the hopelessness and utter subjection of the Lover confronted with Délie's two suns. The sighs are qualified by the adjective *ardentz* linking them with the *ardeur* of line seven and fixing
them for a fleeting moment in the domain of espoir. The *ardentz* also
places the sighs under the sign of fire, thus associating them with
the sun and its effects. However, just as the sun's light brought
darkness, so its fire is followed by extinction of heat as the *ardentz*
*souspirs* are put out by the enemy of fire, water, here in the form
of tears. The tears are, however, not in complete antithesis with

the sighs since they too are *chauldes* and so linked to the heat
projected and inspired by Délie's eyes. Paradoxically, fire is extinguished by another hot element. The adjective *chauldes* thus
stresses the fact that the ultimate cause of this sorrow is Délie
herself, while at the same time insisting on the intensity of both
the Lover's passion and his suffering, which are inspired by the heat
projected from her sun-like eyes.

The relationship between Délie's gaze and the sun's penetrating
rays is the basis for an extended comparison which occupies the
whole of Dizain 386:

> Quand Apollo apres l'Aulbe vermeille
> Poulse le bout de ses rayons dorez,
> Semble a mon œil, qui lors point ne sommeille,
> Veoir les cheveulx, de ce Monde adorez,
> Qui par leurs noudz de mes mortz decorez
> M'ont a ce joug jusqu'a ma fin conduyct.
>    Et quand apres a plaine face il luyt,
> Il m'est advis, que je voy clerement,
> Les yeulx, desquelz la clarté tant me nuyt,
> Qu'elle esblouyt ma veue entierement.

The first six lines of the dizain describes the rising sun in mythological terms and the fact that the sun is presented as Apollo stresses not only his status as god but also his relationship to the moon
and to Délie. Apollo and his rising are portrayed in a dynamic,
aggressive way, as the sunbeams are described as the God's pushing
"le bout de ses rayons dorez." As we noted at the beginning of the
*Délie* in Dizain 12, Scève associates the sun's rays not only with
Délie's eyes but with the traditional conceit of the lady's hair and
its capacity to ensnare and bind the lover. This crossing of two
motifs is used again here by Scève who translates all the phenomena
of nature into his own microcosmic order. Apollo's rays appear to
the Lover as Délie's hair whose tresses are decorated with his suc-
cession of deaths, and which continue to drag him towards death.

The final quatrain of the poem pursues the analogy between
Apollo and Délie by amplifying the power she exercises over him,
and by tracing poetically the progression of her ever-increasing
dominion over him. The mid-day sun conjures up not the vision
of Délie's hair, which had obsessed him in the preceding six lines,

but the dazzling brightness of her eyes, which harm him so much that the excess of light brings temporary blindness.

The devastating effects caused by the full exercise of the power of Délie's gaze are again placed within a mythological and natural framework in Dizain 443.

> Combien qu'a nous soit cause le Soleil
> Que toute chose est tresclerement veue:
> Ce neantmoins pour trop arrester l'œil
> En sa splendeur lon pert soubdain la veue.
>     Mon ame ainsi de son object pourveue
> De tous mes sens me rend abandonné,
> Comme si lors en moy tout estonné
> Semeles fust en presence ravie
> De son Amant de fouldre environné,
> Qui luy ostast par ses esclairs la vie.

The first quatrain of the dizain (divided into a 4-6 configuration) expounds somewhat prosaically a scientific and natural phenomenon: the fact that while the sun normally allows the human eye to see, if the eye tries to contemplate that light directly, it becomes blind. The scientific nature of the utterance is here underlined by the rhymes, which lack Scève's usual richness; *soleil/l'œil,* while being technically acceptable at the time, is nevertheless a marginal rhyme and the use of the past participle *veue* to rhyme with the noun *veue* is obviously a further attempt to make the exposition relatively unpoetic. However, the rhymes do stress the important symbolic relationship between sun and eye, as well as well as bringing out clearly the vital role played by the sense of sight, thanks to the repetition of *veue*.

In fact, *veue* reappears in line five, when the poet turns again to the inner world of the Lover's own universe, in the past participle *pourveue,* which accentuates the visual aspect of the *object* on which the soul now concentrates (as in Dizain 1). The Lover is in a state bordering on death and this is explained with reference to the myth of Semele, who asked to see Jupiter in all his splendour and was consumed by his lightning flashes. What is interesting here is that the Lover's soul is identified with the female protagonist of the myth while Délie is implicitly associated with the ultra-masculine Jupiter, which confirms both her association with the destructively aggressive force of his lightning bolts and her absolute supremacy over the Lover through the power of her gaze.

## 6) *The Eye as Moon*

Sun and Moon are usually thought of as brother and sister in mythology, but in every other aspect as opposites. The sun is bright, aggressive and masculine and symbolises divine illumination and uplifting. The moon is passive, mysterious, feminine; her light is penumbral and funereal in sharp contrast to the direct, dazzling sunlight, and she is often associated with death and the underworld. In the *Délie,* while the moon does sometimes have these traditional symbolical attributes, she is also seen as partaking of the same nature and characteristics as the sun. In other words, her mythological relationship with the sun is exploited by Scève to bring out the similarities rather that the differences between these two celestial bodies. It is interesting to note that the serpent is considered to be a lunar animal, [32] and so the aggressive side of moon imagery, as it is associated with the eyes in *Délie,* is therefore intimately related to the series of poems where the Beloved's eyes are seen as a source of venom, thus implicitly identifying Délie with the serpent (an identification which is, of course, quite explicit in the first dizain).

In Dizain 106, the moon actually eclipses the sun in her capacity to do harm to the Lover and takes a malicious and sadistic pleasure in prolonging his suffering:

> J'attens ma paix du repos de la nuict,
> Nuict refrigere a toute aspre tristesse:
> Mais s'absconsant le Soleil, qui me nuyt,
> Noye avec soy ce peu de ma liesse.
>     Car lors jectant ses cornes la Deesse,
> Qui du bas Ciel esclere la nuict brune,
> Renaist soubdain en moy celle aultre Lune
> Luisante au centre, ou l'Ame à son sejour.
> Qui m'excitant a ma peine commune,
> Me fait la nuict estre un penible jour.

The poem begins with the exposition of what is traditionally considered to be the role of night, that is a consoler, a bringer of rest

---

[32] See Durand, op. cit., p. 101 and pp. 344 ff.

and refreshment. In the torments of love, the protagonist looks forward to this time, when the sun will no longer be present, in order to obtain temporary alleviation of his anguish. However, the sun's setting, far from signaling a mitigation of sadness, takes with it — drowns with it, as the text says in reference to the daily disappearance of the sun beneath the ocean — the last traces of the Lover's happiness, thus plunging him into deeper despair (just as the sun had plunged into the sea). Here it is the relationship rather than the traditional opposition between day and night which is stressed by the rhyme *nuict/nuyt,* the verb *nuyt,* describing the sun's action, is phonetically linked to *nuict,* the domain of the moon. The rising of the moon is strikingly like descriptions elsewhere in the *Délie* of the sun's appearance, and the horns of the crescent moon become aggressive and even diabolic weapons. While the natural moon brings light to the darkness of the *bas Ciel,*[33] the Lover's inner moon also rises on the horizon of his soul, in the very centre of his being, bringing suffering to him even more potently than does the day. The hoped-for transformation expressed in the early part of the poem does not eventuate and the Lover is in a condition of static suffering. Just as the sun was associated with night by the rhyme *nuyt-nuict,* night becomes day in the closing line of the poem, signifying the endless suffering of the love state. While Délie's gaze is not explicitly part of the action of this dizain, the associations of horns, which are aggressive weapons, and with the moon reveals to us the intimate connection between the two.

Should there be any doubt as to the legitimacy of this association, we have only to look seventy dizains further, where in Dizain 176 the details are made quite explicit:

Diane on voit ses deux cornes jecter
Encores tendre, & foiblement naissante:
Et toy des yeux deux rayons forjetter,
La veue basse, & alors moins nuisante.
    Puis sa rondeur elle accomplit luisante:
Et toy ta face elegamment haulsant.
    Elle en apres s'affoiblit descroissant,
Pour retourner une aultrefois novelle:

[33] This is the lowest heaven of the Renaissance universe, the sublunar world in which death and progressive degradation reign.

Et le parfaict de ta beaulté croissant
Dedans mon Cœur tousjours se renovelle.

This poem is in fact a lunar counterpart to Dizain 432 where the action of Délie's eyes was identified with that of the sun. Here the moon is personified in mythological form as Diana and when she rises, her at first weak light is described metaphorically as "ses deux cornes jecter" (a clear recapitulation of the vocabulary of Dizain 106). However, the relationship between these two horns and Délie's eyes is made quite unambiguous as their action parallels that of the rising moon.

The picture of the moon in the first four lines of the dizain is not just that of a rising moon but rather of a new, crescent moon (hence the horns). The second part of the dizain describes the next phase of the moon, the full moon, and here also Délie's action is associated with that of Diana.

Next comes the waning moon which is not here a symbol of declining power but merely a sign of the perpetual renewal associated with the moon's phases. In the same way, Délie's image is constantly being renewed in the Lover's soul and is perpetually exercising her influence over his love-torn life. [34]

This analysis of the principal manifestations of the aggressive eye topos in the *Délie* has demonstrated not only the frequency with which aggressive eye imagery occurs within the work, but also the centrality of such images to the dynamics of Scevian love. Hans Staub's description of Scève as *poète du regard* has proved to be an accurate representation of the importance the poet attributes to the eyes throughout his work. The eye of the Beloved is not only the Prime Mover of Scève's poetic universe, but the power of the Lady's gaze generates the momentum which sustains the Lover's own microcosm, as he is propelled through the various stages of the itinerary of love. It is also the Beloved's eye which brings

---

[34] However, for the more traditional lunar symbolism, see Dizain 305 where Délie provides consolation and joy to the Lover and where her action is compared with that of the moon piercing "l'espaisseur de l'obscurité nuisible" of the night. As we are examining lunar imagery solely in terms of its association with the aggressive eye topos, this other side of Scève's lunar symbolism can only be mentioned in passing as an example of the richness and complexity of his metaphorical universe.

repeated deaths to the Lover, as he surrenders his selfhood to the
Other. However, the organ of vision also brings ressuscitation, res-
surection and a *vita nuova* in and through the Lady. In direct antithesis to the irresistible force of Délie's glance are the passivity and
vulnerability of the Lover's own eyes. They are the necessary antithesis to Délie's aggressive weapons and are the wide open gateway
to his soul, a gateway which constantly betrays him as they allow
her eyebeams to penetrate to the very depths of his being. Yet at
the same time, their treachery is beneficial, for in giving entrance to
Délie's (literally) piercing gaze, they also bring the Lover spiritual
illumination and knowledge of self. In fact, the role of the eyes
is as ambivalent as the nature of love itself, since the eye is both
the principal inspirer of physical desire and at the same time the
only physical organ capable of bringing spiritual insight. Scève's
use of eye imagery functions as one of the principal vehicles of
this duality which is an essential part of love in his poetic universe.
Love is both heaven and hell, death and life, sexual longing and
the illumination of the spirit. The eye captures within its orb all
these apparent contradictions which are not in fact antithetical, but
complementary. The eye not only initiates the poetic journey of
Scève's Lover, it gives it constant impetus. Its workings are also a
reflection in miniature of the movement of the whole work, a microcosm of the *Délie*.

# CONCLUSION

THIS EXCURSION into the various manifestations of the aggressive eye topos in sixteenth century Lyonnais poetry has revealed the vitality, the variety and the sophistication with which the topos and its associated imagery was used. With the exception of Pernette Du Guillet, who appears to have extracted the substance of the topos without having adopted all its forms, and of Pontus de Tyard, who has done precisely the opposite, the Lyonnais poets use all the elements which the topos had acquired since Greek antiquity. They accord it a privileged place in their exploration and representation of love, enriching it with neo-platonic aspirations but without ever removing it entirely from the sphere of sensual love. Indeed a Freudian analysis of the topos would undoubtedly find its sexual connotations to be preponderant. The arrow or other pointed weapon, the serpent, the lightning flash, all these combined with verbs expressing piercing and penetration have phallic overtones which reveal an underlying and perhaps not entirely unconscious sexualisation of the love experience. While it may at first appear strange that when a male poet is treating love, it is the Lady who is the aggressor and who possesses attributes normally considered to be masculine, it should be remembered that in such a framework, the Lady is almost always associated with the Gods and so partakes of their superior powers. She is not simply a woman, but Woman elevated to the status of a cosmic and divine principle. In this context, it is important to realise that if the Lady's eye is associated with the masculine symbolism of the sun, the eye is also a common symbol for the female genital organs,[1] so that the sexuality of the

---

[1] See for example Waldemar Deonna, *Le symbolisme de l'œil* (Paris, 1965), p. 68.

eye assumes an androgynous character which engulfs the fictional
protagonist in male-produced love poetry. The same problem does
not, of course, arise for Labé and Du Guillet who are within the
"norms" of the traditional male-female erotic relationship, and yet
as far as the poetic tradition within which they write is concerned,
their stance as female poets becomes ambiguous, since it is the
male who becomes all-powerful, capricious and cruel in their works
and this is in direct contrast to his usual subservient role in the
Petrarchan (and courtly) scheme of things.

However, if it is naive to disregard the strongly erotic content
of the imagery associated with the aggressive eye topos, it is equally
simplistic to ignore or to minimise the intellectual and spiritual
dimensions of the love experience when it is represented in this
fashion. Although, on the one hand, eyes, arrows and suns can be
interpreted as erotic symbols, we must not forget that the eye also
traditionally brings knowledge ("Voir c'est prendre connaissance du
monde ambiant, c'est 'savoir' "),[2] that the arrow is not only phallic
but also through its ascending motion constitutes a link between
heaven and earth.[3] The arrow is also related to the act of seeing
and of knowing,[4] as well as to the lightning flash which represents
not only divine wrath but also divine illumination. The sun, of
course, is also the eye of the universe, a mythological divinity in
its own right, a symbol of God and heavenly knowledge at the same
time as it symbolises the heat of earthly passion. And yet if the
aggressive eye topos represents in miniature the ambiguity, ambivalence and paradox of love, it should be remembered that such a
union of opposites, the *coincidentia oppositorum* of which we spoke
in reference to Scève's verse, is one of the most fundamental ways
of expressing the reality of the divine,[5] so the love experience
presented by the Lyonnais poets is, in some sense at least, a quest

---

[2] Ibid., pp. 1-2.

[3] Gilbert Durant, *Les structures anthropologiques de l'imaginaire* (Paris:
P.U.F., 1963), pp. 136-138.

[4] "...la flèche, la *sagitta,* n'est-elle pas de même racine que le verbe
*sagire* qui signifie 'percevoir rapidement', et là encore étymologiquement parlant
le sens propre n'est-il pas la concrétisation d'un sens figuré? La flèche (...)
serait symbole du savoir rapide." Ibid., p. 137.

[5] "La *coincidentia oppositorum* est l'une des manières les plus archaïques
par lesquelles se soit exprimé le paradoxe de la réalité divine," Mircea Eliade,
*Traité d'histoire de la religion* (Paris: Payot, 1949), p. 358.

for knowledge and for the divine, while still retaining a strongly sensual dimension. It can be seen as a relative of, or perhaps a counterpart to, mystical religious poetry which explores the relationship between God and Man by using a highly erotic and ambiguous vocabulary.

In addition to its cosmic aspect, the aggressive eye topos has a psychological dimension which is closely akin to certain areas of investigation in modern psychology. Although the arrow imagery which describes the Beloved's glance and the lethal character associated with it, may appear "artificial" and "precious" to a twentieth century reader (at least such is the reaction of most modern readers when they first encounter it), the aggressive eye topos is in fact a statement about the power and influence which the eyes and the act of looking exercise on human behaviour. Sartre, in *L'Etre et le néant*,[6] has made some well-known and perceptive comments on the Other's glance and its effect on the Subject and his environment. Psychologists have recently been devoting considerable attention to the question of eye contact and its consequences on personal relationships, intimacy and aggression. Several recent studies of the problem show that, in fact, the aggressive eye topos has a curious "relevance" to modern preoccupations in this sphere. In a study entitled "Eye-Contact, Distance and Affiliation," Argyle and Dean point out the importance of eye contact in total interpersonal communication:

> Without eye contact (EC), people do not feel that they are fully in communication. Simmel has described it as 'a wholly new and unique union between two people,' and remarked that it represents the most perfect reciprocity in the entire field of human relationship.'[7]

Later in the article they deal with various functions of eye contact and refer to the findings of Ronald Laing.[8] The latter, interestingly enough, uses imagery which is a distant echo of the type of metaphor we associate with the aggressive eye topos:

---

[6] Jean-Paul Sartre, *L'Etre et le néant* (Paris, 1943).
[7] Michael Argyle and Janet Dean, "Eye-Contact, Distance and Affiliation," *Sociometry*, vol. 28, 1965, p. 289.
[8] Ronald Laing, *The Self and Others* (London: Tavistock, 1960), chap. 8.

Some patients, according to Laing, lack adequate feelings of self-regard and ego-identity, and have a great desire to be seen, in order to be 'loved and confirmed as a person.' Some people want to be seen and EC is the proof that they are being seen. Others do not want to be seen, and feel *'impaled before the glance of another,'* feel they are depersonalized or *turned to stone by becoming an object for another's perception.* [9]

Just as the eyebrow in Scève's *blason* was the sign of acceptance or rejection by the Beloved, so psychologists have seen eye contact as bearing the same kind of non-verbal message:

If A gazes at B, this will have a different impact, depending on his facial expression. If there is EC, both may know that A's attitude to B is one of sexual attraction, friendship, hate, dominance or submission. [10]

Another psychological research team reports a similar correlation between eye contact and feelings of attraction toward another person, particularly if the two people involved were of the opposite sex:

These studies indicate that the relationship between eye contact and interpersonal attraction is even more complex that earlier research has implied. Higher levels of eye contact elicit less attraction only when same-sex dyads are in high-intimacy situations. When *personal* positive evaluations were made with high eye contact, both female-female and male-male dyads reported less attraction than in comparable conditions of high eye contact with impersonal positive evaluations; however, with cross-sex dyads using a female confederate and a male subject, a higher level of eye contact elicited more attraction. [11]

As a further indication that the various elements of the aggressive eye topos correspond not only to certain contemporary areas of psychological investigations but also to some constant preoc-

[9] Argyle and Dean, op. cit., p. 292, underlinings ours.
[10] Ibid.
[11] Larry Scherwitz and Robert Helmreich, "Interactive Effects of Eye Contact and Verbal Content on Interpersonal Attraction in Dyads," *Journal of Personality and Social Psychology*, vol. 25, no. 1 (1965), pp. 13-14.

cupations of the human psyche, we also wish to quote in its entirety a letter to Dr. Peter Steincrohn and his reply, which appeared recently in the "Doctor Says" column of a large daily newspaper:

> *Question:* I blame my problem on eyes — mine and those of another. I am a married woman with children, and was absolutely not looking for another man. But — BOOM! — There it is. My age is 35.
>
> It (whatever IT may be) seems to be transmitted from the eye and through the eyes to the nervous system of another. I experience this feeling strongly whenever our eyes meet. But I think I can actually feel, even when my back is turned, that his eyes are on me. This man is married also, and isn't flirting, but just looking — as I am.
>
> Words between us have been only about merchandise I am buying and never about how either of us feels. Of this feeling, we have never spoken, but I sense that he is experiencing the same thing I am. He is on my mind constantly. In fact, I begin to find myself imagining what it would be like to be with him.
>
> How does one turn this off? This must be the way many extramarital affairs begin. Where does it come from? What sets it off? Please try to explain it medically. Just what is there in the eye contact to produce such a problem?
>
> *Answer:* I presume you come to me for advice because you really believe that for some physiological reason, or for reason of some chemical interaction, the eyes (and the eyes alone) are the guilty culprits. I wish I knew the answer.
>
> I'm not being facetious or putting you down when I say I do not have the wisdom of Cupid. I think you could get much better practical advice from other columnists who deal daily with similar problems.
>
> All I can offer as a doctor is the fact that the eyes themselves are not to blame. If you really want the problem resolved, better discuss it with your family doctor or with a marriage counselor. Better now, early — than too late. [12]

The inclusion of this rather simplistic and simple-minded letter from such an unscholarly source as a daily newspaper (and not even

---

[12] Peter Steincrohn, "Doctor Says," *The Evening Bulletin* (Philadelphia, October 8, 1975), p. 67.

the *New York Times* at that!) is not intended to be frivolous in spite of its (I presume) unconscious humour, nor is it an attempt to accord some kind of factitious relevance to a time-honoured literary topos which is now largely abandoned by modern poets. It is, however, intended to show that if the physiological and scientific framework we now use to explain the act of seeing and the state of being-in-love are different and perhaps more sophisticated than those of the Renaissance, the manner in which love is engendered and transmitted is still very much a mystery. If the explanation provided by the aggressive eye topos is now considered to be physiologically unsound, the fact that a twentieth century housewife, presumably with no knowledge of the Greek literary tradition nor of the efflux theory of vision can unconsciously have recourse to terminology which could, with some stylistic changes, find itself in a Renaissance treatise on love, does show that the aggressive eye topos has a psychological relevance which transcends its literal form. While on the surface it may appear to us to be scientifically infantile, it does take into account the suddenness, the mystery and the irresistibility many have experienced in love and does justice to the special place the eyes and the love-glance have always been accorded in accounts of the love relationship. To some extent, the aggressive eye topos may and perhaps should be seen not just as a literary theme but as imbued with the archetypal nature we associate with mythology. This would help to explain why the housewife of the daily newspaper instinctively had recourse to it and why the account of the role played by the eyes in love offered by Dr. Jacques Ferrand (the seventeenth century Parisian physician we referred to in Chapter I) may well be more profound and satisfying that the prosaic, if scientifically sound, explanation of his modern-day counterpart, for as we have seen:

Si nescis, oculi sunt in amore duces.

# BIBLIOGRAPHY

1) *Literary and Philosophical Works Containing Eye Imagery (from Antiquity to the time of the 'Ecole Lyonnaise')*

Aeschylus, *Agamemnon,* ed. E. Fraenkel (Oxford, 1950).

Anacreaon, *Odes,* trans. Thomas Moore (London, 1860).

Andreas Capellanus, *The Art of Courtly Love,* ed. and trans. J. J. Perry (New York, 1959).

Apollonius Rhodius, *Argonautica,* trans. R. C. Seaton (Harvard U. P., 1961).

Arberry, A. J. (ed.), *Moorish Poetry* (Cambridge, 1953).

———, *The Seven Odes* (London, 1957).

———, *Arabic Poetry* (Cambridge, 1965).

Ariosto, Ludovico, *Opere,* ed. A. Racheli (Trieste, 1857).

———, *Orlando furioso,* ed. S. Debenedetti (Bari, 1928).

Arnaut de Mareuil, *Les poésies lyriques,* ed. R. Johnston (Geneva, 1935).

Averroës, *Epitome of Parva Naturalia,* ed. H. Blumberg (Cambridge, 1961).

Bembo, Pietro, *Gli Asolani* (Vinegia, 1515).

———, *Rime* (Venezia, 1729).

Bernart de Ventadorn, *Chansons d'amour,* ed. Moshé Lazar (Paris, 1966).

Boccaccio, Giovanni, *Fiammetta,* ed. G. Gigli (Strasburg: Biblioteca Italiana, n. d.).

*Book of the Thousand Nights and a Night,* trans. R. Burton (New York, 1962).

Bouelles, Charles de, *Liber de intellectu, Liber de sensu* (Paris, 1510).

Burton, Robert, *The Anatomy of Melancholy,* ed. F. Dell and P. Jordan-Smith (London, 1931).

Castiglione, Baldesar, *Il Cortegiano* (Torino, 1955).

Catullus, *Catullus, Tibullus and Pervigilium Veneris* (Cambridge, 1962).

Charles d'Orléans, *Poésies complètes,* ed. C. Héricault (Paris, n. d.).

Chrestien de Troyes, *Cligès,* ed. A. Micha (Paris, 1957).

Dante, *La vita nuova,* ed. N. Sapegno (Florence, 1931).

Ebreo, Leone, *Dialoghi d'Amore* (Bari, 1929).

*Enéas, Le Roman d',* ed. Jacques Salverda de Grave (Halle, 1891).

Ferrand, Jacques, *De la maladie de l'amour* (Paris, 1623).

Folquet de Marseille, *Le troubadour Folquet de Marseille,* ed. Stanislaw Stronski (Geneva: Slatkine, 1968).

*Greek Romances of Heliodorus, Longus and Achilles Tatius,* trans. R. Smith (London, 1855).

Heroët, Antoine, *La parfaicte Amye* in *Œuvres poétiques,* ed. F. Gohin (Paris, 1909).
Hesiod, *The Works and Days and the Theogony,* trans. R. Lattimore (Ann Arbor, 1970).
Lemaire de Belges, Jean, *Œuvres,* ed. J. Stecher (Louvain, 1885).
Lucian, *Œuvres complètes,* trans. E. Talbot (Paris, 1866).
Lycophron, *The Alexandria,* ed. G. W. Mooney (London, 1921).
*Medallions from Anyte of Tegea, Meleager of Gadara, the Anacreontea,* trans. Richard Aldington (London, 1930).
Molinet, Jean, *Les Faictz et Dictz* (Paris, 1936-39).
Musaeus, *Hero and Leander,* trans. G. Chapman (Shaftesbury, 1936).
Ovid, *Metamorphoses and The Art of Love,* trans. F. Miller (London, 1916).
Petrarca, Francesco, *Canzoniere,* ed. G. Contini (Torino, 1964).
Pindar, *The Odes,* trans. John Sandys (Cambridge, 1957).
Plato, *Phaedrus,* trans. R. Hackforth (Cambridge, 1952).
———, *Timaeus,* ed. and trans. R. D. Archer (London, 1888).
Pliny, *Natural History,* trans. H. Rackham (Cambridge and London, 1940).
*Poeti del Duecento,* ed. G. Contini (Milano, n. d.).
Propertius, *Works,* trans. H. E. Butler (Cambridge and London, 1958).
*Roman de la rose,* ed. F. Lecoy (Paris, 1968).
Saint Gelays, Melin de, *Œuvres complètes* (Paris, 1873).
Serafino dall'Aquila, *Opere* (Bologna, 1894).
Speroni, Sperone, *Opere* (Venezia, 1740).
Vidal, Peire, *Les poésies,* ed. J. Anglade (Paris, 1913).
Virgil, *Eclogues, Georgics, Aeneid I-VI,* trans. H. R. Fairclough (Cambridge and London, 1967).

2) *General Critical Works*

Argyle, M. and Dean, J., "Eye contact distance and affiliation," *Sociometry,* 1965, 28, pp. 289-304.
Bensimon, Marc, "The significance of eye imagery in the Renaissance from Bosch to Montaigne," *Yale French Studies,* 19, #47, pp. 266-290.
Bosco, Umberto, *Francesco Petrarca* (Bari, 1965).
Calcaterra, Carlo, *Il Petrarca e il petrarchismo* (Milano, 1965).
Cline, Ruth H., "Heart and Eyes," *Romance Philology,* 1971-72, vol. 25, pp. 263-297.
Colby, Alice M., *The Portrait in Twelfth Century French Literature* (Geneva, 1965).
Colonia, P. de, *Histoire littéraire de la ville de Lyon* (Lyon, 1728-30).
Couat, André, *Alexandrian poetry under the first three Ptolemies,* trans. James Loeb (London, 1931).
Day, Archibald, *The Origins of the Latin Love Elegy* (Oxford, 1938).
Deonna, Waldemar, *Le symbolisme de l'œil* (Paris, 1965).
Dimler, Richard J., "The arrow in F. Spee's Tructznachtigall," *Classical Folia,* v. 26, pp. 279-288.
Ellsworth, P. C. and Carlsmith, J. M., "Effects of eye contact and verbal content on affective response to a dyadic interaction," *Journal of Personal and Social Psychology,* 1968, #10, pp. 15-20.
Festugière, Jean, *La philosophie de l'amour de Marsile Ficin* (Paris, 1941).
Fleming, John, *The 'Roman de la Rose' — A Study in Allegory and Iconography* (Princeton, 1969).

Forster, L., *The Icy Fire* (Cambridge, 1969).
Funk and Wagnall, *Standard Dictionary of Folklore, Mythology and Legend* (New York, 1949).
Hutton, James, *The Greek Anthology in France* (New York, 1946).
*Jardin de Plaisance et Fleur de rhetoricque, Le* (Lyon, n. d.).
Jeanroy, A., *La poésie des troubadours* (Toulouse, 1934).
Klibansky, R., *The Continuity of the Platonic Tradition* (London, 1939).
Kolb, Herbert, *Der Begriff der Minne* (Tübingen, 1958).
Luck, Georg, *The Latin Love Elegy* (New York, 1960).
Lyall, C. J., *Ancient Arabic Poetry* (New York, 1930).
Menestrier, François, *L'art des emblèmes* (Lyons, 1626).
Merrill, R. V., "Eros and Anteros," *Speculum,* 1944, XIX, pp. 265-284.
Meylan, E. F., "L'évolution de la notion d'amour platonique," *Humanisme et Renaissance,* 1938, V.
Nicholson, R. A., *Studies in Islamic Poetry* (Cambridge, 1921).
Pearson, A. C., "Phrixus and Demodice," *Classical Review,* 1910, XXIII, pp. 256 ff.
Pérès, Henri, *La poésie andalouse en arabe classique au XIe siècle* (Paris, 1953).
Perry, T. Anthony, "Leone Ebreo's *Dialoghi d'amore,*" *PMLA,* 1973, #88, pp. 1173-1179.
Piéri, Marius, *Le pétrarquisme au XVIe siècle* (Marseille, 1895).
Praz, Mario, *Studies in Seventeenth Century Imagery* (London, 1947).
Robin, L., *La théorie platonicienne de l'amour* (Paris, 1908).
Scherwitz, L. and Helmreich, R., "Interactive effects of eye contact on interpersonal attraction in dyads," *Journal of Personal and Social Psychology,* 1973, #25.
Shaw, J. E., *Guido Cavalcanti's Theory of Love* (Toronto, 1949).
Shepard, Odell, *The Lore of the Unicorn* (London, 1930).
Siegel, Rudolph E., *Galen on Sense Perception* (Basel and New York, 1970).
Starobinski, Jean, *L'œil vivant* (Paris, 1961).
Ullah, Najib, *Islamic Literature* (New York, 1963).
Vance, Eugene, "Le combat érotique chez Chrétien de Troyes," *Poétique,* 1972, #12.
Vianey, J., *Le pétrarquisme en France au XVIe siècle* (Montpellier, 1909).
Weber, Henri, *La création poétique au XVIe siècle en France* (Paris, 1956).

## 3) Ecole Lyonnaise: Texts and Critical Works

### Pernette Du Guillet:

*Rymes,* ed. Victor E. Graham (Geneva, 1968).
Cottrell, Robert D., "Pernette Du Guillet's *Rymes,*" *Bibliothèque d'Humanisme,* 1969, #31, pp. 553-571.
Griffin, Robert, "Pernette Du Guillet's Response to Scève: a case for abstract love," *Esprit Créateur,* 1965, #5, pp. 110-116.
Saulnier, V.-L., "Etude sur Pernette Du Guillet," *BHR,* 1944, #4.
T. A. Perry, "Pernette Du Guillet's Poetry of Love and Desire," *BHR,* vol. 35, 1973, pp. 259-271.

### Louise Labé:

*Œuvres* (Lyon, 1824).
*Œuvres complètes,* ed. J.-J. Salverda de Grave (Maestricht, 1928).

Chan, Andrea, "Petrarchism and Neoplatonism in Louise Labé's Concept of Happiness," *Australian Journal of French Studies,* XIV, 1977, pp. 213-232.

Guillot, Gérard, *Louise Labé et son œuvre* (Paris, 1962).

Harvey, Lawrence E., *The Aesthetics of the Renaissance Love Sonnet* (Geneva, 1962).

Ruwet, Nicolas, "Analyse structurale d'un poème français," *Linguistics,* January 1964, #3, pp. 62-63.

*Olivier de Magny:*

*Les 102 sonnets des Amours de 1553,* ed. M. S. Whitney (Geneva, 1970).

*Maurice Scève:*

*Délie,* ed. I. D. McFarlane (Cambridge, 1966).

*Œuvres complètes,* ed. Pascal Quignard (Paris, 1974).

Attal, Jean-Pierre, "Etat présent des études scéviennes," *Critique,* Jan. 1960.

Aynard, Joseph, *Les poètes lyonnais précurseurs de la Pléiade* (Paris, 1924).

Baur, Albert, *Maurice Scève et la renaissance lyonnaise* (Paris, 1906).

Béguin, Albert, "La mystique de Maurice Scève," *Confluences,* 1944, pp. 229-243.

Boutang, P., *Commentaire sur 49 dizains de la 'Délie'* (Paris, 1953).

Coleman, Dorothy Gabe, *Maurice Scève Poet of Love* (Cambridge, 1975).

———, "Some notes on Scève and Petrarch," *French Studies,* XIV, 1960, pp. 293-303.

———, "Dizain 104 in Maurice Scève's *Délie,*" *Modern Language Review,* 1963, pp. 215-217.

———, "Scève's choice of the name *Délie,*" *French Studies,* XVIII, 1964, pp. 1-16.

———, "Les Emblesmes dans la *Délie* de Maurice Scève," *Studi francesi,* #22, 1964, pp. 1-15.

———, "Images in Scève's *Délie,*" *Modern Language Review,* LIX, 1964, pp. 375-386.

———, "Propertius, Petrarch and Scève," *Kentucky Romance Quarterly,* XVIII, 1971, pp. 77-89.

Fenoaltea, Doranne, "Three animal images in the *Délie:* new perspectives on Scève's use of Petrarch's *Rime,*" *BHR,* xxxiv, 1972, pp. 413-426.

———, "The poet in nature: sources of Scève's *Délie* in Petrarch's *Rime,*" *French Studies,* XXVI, 1973, pp. 257-270.

Frappier, Jean, "Variations sur le thème du miroir de Bernard de Ventadorn à Maurice Scève," *Cahiers de l'Association Internationale des Etudes Françaises,* vol. 11, 1959.

Giudici, Enzo, *Il Rinascimento a Lione e la 'Délie' di Maurice Scève* (Napoli, 1962).

Greene, Thomas M., "Styles of experience in Scève's *Délie,*" *Yale French Studies,* #47, 1972, pp. 57-75.

Meyers, Odette Sarah, *Le symbole du miroir: point de jonction entre l'œuvre poétique de Pernette du Guillet et la Délie de Maurice Scève,* PhD Thesis, University of California, Riverside, 1971.

Mourgues, Odette de, *Metaphysical, Baroque and Précieux Poetry* (Oxford, 1953).

Mulhauser, Ruth, "The poetic function of the Emblems in *Délie,*" *Esprit Créateur,* #2, 1965.

Niedermann, W., *Versuch über Maurice Scèves Dichtung* (Zürich, 1950).

Perry, T. Anthony, "Délie! An old way of dying (A new hypothesis on Scève's title)," *French Forum,* 1, #1, Jan. 1976, pp. 2-13.

Quignard, Pascal, *La Parole de la 'Délie': essai sur Maurice Scève* (Paris, 1974).

Rigolot, François, "Paronymie et sémantique nominale chez Pétrarque et Scève," in *Poétique et onomastique* (Geneva: Droz, 1977), pp. 105-126.

Risset, Jacqueline, *L'Anagramme du désir. Essai sur la 'Délie' de Maurice Scève* (Rome, 1971).

Runyon, Randolph, "Delivrance: Souffrir non souffrir," *M. L. N.,* May 1973.

Saulnier, V.-L., *Maurice Scève* (Paris, 1948-49).

————, "Maurice Scève et la clarté," *Bulletin de l'Association G. Budé,* nouvelle série 5, June 1948, pp. 96-105.

Staub, Hans, *Le Curieux désir* (Geneva, 1967).

Weber, Henri, *Le langage poétique de Maurice Scève dans la 'Délie'* (Florence, 1948).

*Pontus de Tyard:*

*Erreurs amoureuses,* ed. J. McClelland (Geneva, 1967).